D1592251

For information about

**EFFECTIVE NEGOTIATION
AND MEDIATION:
A LAWYER'S GUIDE**
(looseleaf edition)
by
Paul M. Lisnek

call your West Representative or 1–800–328–9352.

This Guide, part of West's *LAWYERING SKILLS SERIES*, includes forms and additional materials from which this abridged, CLE edition is adapted. To order *Effective Negotiation and Mediation: A Lawyer's Guide*, looseleaf edition, please call West Publishing Company.

1–800–328–9352

WEST PUBLISHING COMPANY
610 Opperman Drive
P.O. Box 64526
St. Paul, MN 55164–0526

DISPUTE RESOLUTION TOOLS FROM WEST

LAWYERING SKILLS SERIES

Effective Negotiation and Mediation: A Lawyer's Guide
Paul M. Lisnek

**Trialbook: A Total System for the Preparation
and Presentation of a Case**
John O. Sonsteng, Roger S. Haydock and James J. Boyd

Depositions: Procedure, Strategy and Technique
Paul M. Lisnek and Michael J. Kaufman

**Effective Client Communication:
A Lawyer's Handbook for Interviewing and Counseling**
Paul M. Lisnek

Federal Civil Trialbook
Cari P. Matthews

Commercial Arbitration with Forms
Robert M. Rodman

Federal Practice & Procedure
Charles Alan Wright, Arthur R. Miller, Mary Kay Kane, Edward H. Cooper,
Richard L. Marcus, Kenneth W. Graham and Victor James Gold

Handbook of Federal Evidence
Michael H. Graham

Trial Advocacy
James Jeans

Photographic Evidence
Charles C. Scott

**Federal Jury Practice and Instructions
Civil and Criminal**
Edward J. Devitt, Charles B. Blackmar, Michael A. Wolff
and Kevin F. O'Malley

Federal Court of Appeals Manual
David G. Knibb

DISPUTE RESOLUTION TOOLS

Federal Civil Judicial Procedure and Rules

Manual for Complex Litigation

Federal Rules of Evidence for United States Courts and
Magistrates

———

WESTLAW® and WEST BOOKS
The Ultimate Research System

———

To order any of these West practice tools, call your West Representative or 1–800–328–9352.

November, 1992

A LAWYER'S GUIDE TO EFFECTIVE NEGOTIATION AND MEDIATION

CLE Edition

By

PAUL MICHAEL LISNEK, J.D., Ph.D.
Vice President and Director of Mediator Training,
Lawyers Mediation Service Corporation
Vice President and Director of Academics,
National Institute for Legal Education
Former Assistant Dean and Professor
Loyola University of Chicago School of Law

ST. PAUL, MINN.
WEST PUBLISHING CO.
1993

WEST'S COMMITMENT TO THE ENVIRONMENT

In 1906, West Publishing Company began recycling materials left over from the production of books. This began a tradition of efficient and responsible use of resources. Today, more than 95% of our legal books and 70% of our college texts are printed on acid-free, recycled paper consisting of 50% new paper pulp and 50% paper that has undergone a de-inking process. We also use soy-based inks to print many of our books. West recycles nearly 22,650,000 pounds of scrap paper annually—the equivalent of 187,500 trees. Since the 1960s, West has devised ways to capture and recycle waste inks, solvents, oils, and vapors created in the printing process. We also recycle plastics of all kinds, wood, glass, corrugated cardboard, and batteries, and have eliminated the use of styrofoam book packaging. We at West are proud of the longevity and the scope of our commitment to the environment.

West pocket parts are printed on recyclable paper and can be collected and recycled with newspapers. Staples do not have to be removed because recycling companies use magnets to extract staples during the recycling process.

Lisnek Effective Negotiation & Mediation
CLE Edition

This book is dedicated to:

The loving memory of my aunt, Dalcy Jorbin;
the strength and spirit of my uncle, David Jorbin;
the perseverance and will of my brother, Richard Lisnek.

*

PREFACE TO CLE EDITION

Perhaps no topic fascinates the lawyer more than the art of negotiation. The complexities of determining where best to open one's position, the realities and likelihood of where the process will go, and the uncertainty of everyone else's needs and strategies requires an acuity for understanding people. Yet, lawyers have little training in how to read and handle the dynamics of negotiation.

As the process of litigation has grown to be exceedingly more complex over recent years, so the backlog of cases seems to increase each day. Clients search for better roads to resolution, those that offer expediency, economy and peace of mind. As alternative dispute resolution becomes an increasingly used mechanism for case management, clients become intrigued with the possibilities. This book places a focus on mediation because it is essentially the only form of commonly used ADR procedures that requires resolution through the mutual consent of the parties. There is no third party who imposes any decision or findings of fact on the parties; only a facilitator who works closely to gain the trust of the parties so they can all come to realize the areas of mutual agreement that exist between them.

As lawyers come to gain a better understanding of mediation, and begin to experience the process under the guidance of a skilled mediator, they will soon come to realize that no other dispute resolution process offers the rewards that mediation provides. These rewards include the preservation of business, personal and social relationships, confidence in and a greater likelihood of adherence to the terms of an agreement that the parties have crafted, and earlier resolution of legal matters.

The tie between negotiation and mediation is clear enough: negotiation skills provide the foundation for every type of settlement effort. Even the cooperative nature of mediation requires a keen sense of awareness and strategy grounded in negotiation ability.

This book is an *abridged* version of the complete text, *Effective Negotiation and Mediation: A Lawyer's Guide* (West Publishing, 1992). This volume presents only the essential components of the complete book. Its intended use is as materials for a continuing legal education program on these topics. I encourage you to review the book from which these materials are gathered to gain a more complete understanding of the processes and a complete set of planning and strategy forms.

For this initial journey into the strategies of negotiation and mediation, I wish you insight and a thirst for more knowledge.

PAUL M. LISNEK

Chicago, IL
December, 1992

*

PUBLISHER'S NOTE

A Lawyer's Guide to Effective Negotiation and Mediation, CLE edition, by Paul M. Lisnek, is designed for use in CLE programs. This CLE edition is the abridged version of the looseleaf edition, and the section numbering from the looseleaf edition has been retained in the CLE edition.

For information about, or to order, the CLE edition or the looseleaf edition of *Effective Negotiation and Mediation: A Lawyer's Guide,* please call West Publishing Company at 1–800–328–9352.

*

ACKNOWLEDGEMENTS

It should come as no surprise that the creation of any book is the culmination of countless months of research, creativity, drafting, editing and then repeating the entire process over again. This text is no different and there are several people to whom a great debt of gratitude is owed.

Ted A. Donner, and Michael Simon served as my research assistants during their law school years. Their extensive effort to assist in the review and incorporation of research was invaluable. Without that effort, there would clearly be no book. Their reflections and reactions throughout the course of this book's development likewise kept me on the proper path to present text and forms that would be both relevant and practical.

Jeremy S. Karlin assisted as deadlines approached with essential citation gathering and confirmation. When I could no longer keep my eyes open, Jeremy kept WESTLAW operating and insured an up-to-the-minute inclusion of relevant state statutes.

I also extend appreciation to my colleagues on the faculty of Loyola University of Chicago School of Law, where my over six years as the assistant dean remain a motivating and positive memory and force behind my writing. Special appreciation goes to my colleague and friend, Michael Mendelson, who put up with quite a lot with this boss during the process. I extend heartfelt appreciation to my staff: Reneé Hillman, my Vice-President and Director of Client Relations, and Richard Anton, administrative assistant extraordinaire.

My friends and colleagues at Pepperdine University's Institute for Dispute Resolution, including Professors Randy Lowry and Peter Robinson and Joan Winstel who "force me to teach" in a classroom on the ocean in Malibu as a visiting professor each summer.

My colleagues with the Lawyers Mediation Service Corporation, specifically, Ernest and Marcia Cohen from the administrative office in Tucson, Professor Paul Marcus, Fern Billet, and Barbara Holtzman, all of whom read portions of the text with a careful eye. Our joint endeavor to train and use some of the country's finest mediators (law professors, deans, retired judges and seasoned litigators) was a driving force behind the inclusion of mediation as a major part of this text.

Other practical insights for this text emanate from my continued work with Joyce Tsongas, Dennis Brooks, Art Monson and my other colleagues at Portland, Oregon based Tsongas Associates, certainly one of the finest groups of trial consultants in the country, creating strategy for negotiation and mediation with some of our finest lawyers; from William Flannery and Julie Eichorn, my colleagues at the WJF Institute based in Austin, Texas who teach quality client service, negotiation and client development strategies with the top law firms in the nation; and from Chris

ACKNOWLEDGEMENTS

M. Salamone and Anthony Salamone, my colleagues at the National Institute for Legal Education and the National Law Program, who work closely with me each summer to incorporate the spirit of the message of this text into the education of young adults and future lawyers through an excellent pre-legal educational curriculum.

Certainly, many people (some lawyers, and some actually *not*) have played a role in my personal growth and stability throughout the creation of this book, a difficult task that had to be balanced as I travel and teach around the country: in Chicago, sister-in-law Judy Kien, Steve Pearson, Arnie Pierson, Raymond Massey, Domini Hunt, Al Menotti, Bob Anderson, Cindy Raymond, Robert Bell, Kenneth Fischbein, Emilio Machado, Michael Menefee, Danny Tag and Elizabeth Braham, Steve Rubin, Tony and Cathy Parrilli, and Marlene Rubin; in the midwest, Paul Fogelberg, Laurie Hennen, Connie Hendrickson, Larry Bushong, Barbara Blaser, Barry Arthur Litwin, Janice Wexler, and along the coasts, Steve Gorman, Marcia Moulton, Ben Haglund and Peter Vannucci. Not many people can boast of such a powerful support network and I am proud to call you all friends.

Perhaps it is redundant to express my appreciation for the never-ending support and love of my parents, Seymour and Sandy Lisnek, in each of the books I write. However, as the years go on, each day I share with them seems to become more precious and important; I continually recognize the support, encouragement and faith they have placed in me over the years. Since no words seem to me an adequate expression of my love for them, let me simply add in this personal way, "Thanks for being a part of everything I have accomplished and ever will be fortunate enough to achieve; and Mom and Dad, know that I will always love you."

This is the third book I have written in this practice skills series and I am dedicated to creating texts that are practical and relevant for litigators. My extensive lecturing schedule around the country has provided me with the opportunity to learn first hand how useful and used these texts are by those practitioners who purchase them. It is heart warming to learn that so many people have come to rely on the forms and structure of these books both for preparation and to resolve matters which need a quick answer. In an ongoing effort to insure that future editions contain the material and approach most desired by lawyers, I invite your comments and suggestions. Please feel free to write to me through West Publishing Company, or directly at:

612 North Michigan Avenue
Suite 217
Chicago, Illinois 60611
(312) 248–5600

I wish you continuing awareness and an increase in your negotiation and mediation skill levels that exceeds even your own high expectations!

ABOUT THE AUTHOR

PAUL M. LISNEK is a nationally recognized speaker and trainer on lawyering skills. He is formerly the assistant dean of Loyola University of Chicago School of Law where he taught negotiation, professional responsibility and pretrial litigation. He is an adjunct professor of law with Pepperdine University Institute for Dispute Resolution. Dr. Lisnek is currently the Vice President and Director of Mediator Training for Lawyers Mediation Service Corporation, the nation's only national network of law school deans, law professors, judges and seasoned litigators who work as mediators. He is also a mediator for the Cook County Court Mediation Program. He is also a senior trial consultant with Tsongas Associates, specializing in witness preparation and jury research, and past president of the American Society of Trial Consultants. He serves on the faculty of the WJF Institute, teaching quality service to lawyers.

Dean Lisnek holds a law degree and Ph.D. in legal communication from the University of Illinois. He holds a master practitioner certification in neurolinguistic programming, a communication science Dr. Lisnek incorporates into his lectures and training. He lectures across the country on lawyering and communication skills, including negotiation, mediation, depositions, interviewing and counseling, and jury psychology. He is a commissioner on and is chairperson of the inquiry panel of the Illinois Attorney Disciplinary Commission. He is host of an award winning television talk show in Chicago, "Inside Your Government," and has served as a guest commentator on "Court T.V." He is also director of academics of the National Institute for Legal Education, which presents educational programs for people interested in pursuing a career in law.

Paul Lisnek's previous publications by West Publishing Company include: *Depositions: Procedures, Techniques and Strategy* (with Michael Kaufman) and *Effective Client Communication—A Lawyer's Handbook for Interviewing and Counseling*.

*

WESTLAW® ELECTRONIC RESEARCH GUIDE

1. Coordinating Legal Research with WESTLAW

Effective Negotiation and Mediation provides essential information dealing with clients and witnesses. WESTLAW provides additional resources. This guide will assist your use of WESTLAW to supplement this treatise.

2. Databases

A database is an aggregation of documents with one or more features in common. A database may contain statutes, court decisions, administrative materials, or commentaries. Every database has its own identifier. WESTLAW does contain the ABA Ethics Opinions (LS–ABAEO); the ABA Rules of Professional Conduct (LS–MRPC); and several states ethics opinions (MLS–EO). The WESTLAW Directory is a comprehensive listing of databases, with information about each database, including the types of documents each contains.

3. Updating Statutes

WESTLAW statutory databases may be used to find statutes and to ascertain whether a particular statute has been amended after a bound volume or pocket part of the statutes was printed. Check the WESTLAW Directory to see if the desired statutory database is available and its coverage.

4. Key Number Search

WESTLAW may be used to search any topic and key number in West's Key Number System. To retrieve cases with at least one headnote classified to the topic Attorney and Client ☞32(g), sign on to a caselaw database and enter:

45k32(g)

The topic name Attorney and Client is replaced by its numerical equivalent 45 and the ☞ by the letter k. A list of topics and their numerical equivalents is in the WESTLAW Reference Manual and is also available in the WESTLAW Directory.

5. Retrieving a Cited Case

WESTLAW's FIND command can be used to quickly retrieve a cited case. Simply enter a command in this form:

fi 108 S.Ct. 1916

6. Using Insta-Cite® for Case History and Parallel Citations

Insta-Cite® may be used to find any parallel citations and the history of a reported case. Enter a command in this form:

ic 98 S.Ct. 1912

All parallel cites will be displayed together with the history of the case reported at 98 S.Ct. 1912.

7. Shepardizing® a Case with WESTLAW

Shepard's® Citations may be displayed for a reported case. Enter a command in this form:

sh 407 So.2d 595

The Shepard's information for the case reported at 407 So.2d 595 will be displayed.

8. Additional Information

The information provided above illustrates some of the ways WESTLAW can complement research using this treatise. However, this brief overview illustrates only some of the power of WESTLAW. The full range of WESTLAW search techniques is available to support your research from this series. Please consult the WESTLAW manual for additional information.

For information about subscribing to WESTLAW, please call 1–800–328–0109.

SUMMARY OF CONTENTS

PROLOGUE: INTERACTION DYNAMICS

BOOK ONE.   THE ART OF NEGOTIATION

PART I.   PREPARING TO NEGOTIATE

PART II.   CONDUCTING THE NEGOTIATION

BOOK TWO.   MEDIATION—THE ROAD TO RESOLUTION

*

* Chapters denoted with an asterisk can be found in the looseleaf edition only.

TABLE OF CONTENTS

* Chapters and sections denoted with an asterisk can be found in the looseleaf edition only.

* Chapters and sections denoted with an asterisk can be found in the looseleaf edition only.

TABLE OF CONTENTS

PART II.   CONDUCTING THE NEGOTIATION

* Chapters and sections denoted with an asterisk can be found in the looseleaf edition only.

BOOK TWO.   MEDIATION—THE ROAD
TO RESOLUTION

* Chapters and sections denoted with an asterisk can be found in the looseleaf edition
only.

* Chapters and sections denoted with an asterisk can be found in the looseleaf edition only.

 * Chapters and sections denoted with an asterisk can be found in the looseleaf edition only.

BOOK ONE.   THE ART OF NEGOTIATION

PART I

PREPARING TO NEGOTIATE

Chapter 2

THE NEGOTIATION PROCESS

Table of Sections

WESTLAW Electronic Research

See WESTLAW Electronic Research Guide preceding the Summary of Contents.

Notes

§ 2.1 Measuring Lawyer Effectiveness in Legal Negotiation

Lawyers negotiate contract terms, case settlements and accompanying conditions nearly every day. Yet this

---

A Lawyer's Guide to Effective Negotiation and Mediation, CLE edition, is the abridged version of the looseleaf edition
designed for use in CLE programs. The section and form numbering from the looseleaf edition
have been retained in the CLE edition.

skill, used so extensively in practice, is emphasized little in legal education. Perhaps the failure to focus education on these skills represents an old belief that negotiation cannot be taught, but must be experienced; maybe it's a reflection of the seemingly ever-present tension between the teaching of substantive law courses and a resistance to incorporating the practical into the standard legal education.

Regardless, exposure to the process and theory of negotiation is the essence of legal analysis and strategy. A theoretical understanding of the area of law involved is certainly prerequisite to an effective negotiation, but without the practical sense of the psychology of negotiation, even the most substantively informed lawyers will not achieve the best terms for their clients.

Certainly, the teaching of negotiation skills is not an easy task because each lawyer has his or her own style of negotiating. Different negotiators will approach the same case differently and one lawyer may approach a particular negotiation situation in a variety of ways, depending on their strategic analysis of the case and negotiation environment. Thus it appears to be a difficult task to teach negotiation techniques that would work for every lawyer.

The disparity of lawyer negotiation skills across situations is evidenced by the inconsistency in settlement amounts and terms achieved by lawyers in similar (or even the same) cases. For example, a study simulation conducted in Des Moines, Iowa, brought twenty pairs of volunteer lawyers together to negotiate the same set of hypothetical facts of a personal injury lawsuit. Of the fourteen lawyers who were willing to disclose their settlement results, three did not achieve a settlement. The settlements for the eleven pairs who reached agreement ranged from $15,000 to $95,000. The initial offers based on the hypothetical facts and made by Defendants ranged from $3,000 to $50,000; the Plaintiff's initial demands all based on the same facts, ranged from $32,000 to $675,000. Gerald R. Williams, *Legal Negotiation and Settlement* (West Publishing, 1986) at 7. Simply put, different law-

A Lawyer's Guide to Effective Negotiation and Mediation, CLE edition, is the abridged version of the looseleaf edition designed for use in CLE programs. The section and form numbering from the looseleaf edition have been retained in the CLE edition.

yers value a case differently; they exercise different approaches in the settlement negotiation.

Form 2–1 assists the lawyer to value a case, a task often enhanced through discussion and reflection between firm associates in a law firm setting. There is no substitute for careful research and consideration when evaluating a case for settlement. It is the evaluation that becomes the basis from which many lawyers plan and pursue settlement negotiations.

The form requires a look at the actual costs incurred in a lawsuit and a view of the potential components for other damages. It is difficult to put a dollar figure on pain and suffering or speculating on future lost business, but negotiation requires such insight. It is from these estimates, and the support that can be created for them, that positions are discussed, compromised or hardened.

The form, if completed properly, assists lawyers in developing starting points from which negotiation can more effectively begin. Certainly, the numbers may be adjusted based on information learned during the course of discovery, investigation or negotiation; in fact, Form 2–1 anticipates and provides for such expected adjustments. The negotiation process requires flexibility and a fluid sense that permits the negotiators to shift from stated positions as the discussion might necessitate.

In many ways, the considerations raised by Form 2–1 may be among the most important in the book. A lawyer who enters a negotiation or mediation session without knowing the information specified on the form is subject to the strategies and skill reflected in the careful preparation of the opponent. It is almost a certainty that the unprepared lawyer will not fare well in a negotiation.

Determining what it means to "fare well" is not an easy task. Many lawyers assume that any negotiation ending with the highest gain has been the best session. Certainly, the final results are but one component of the negotiation equation of success. However, in reality, it is difficult to evaluate any negotiation based solely on its final terms. In fact, if the parties are dissatisfied with the

A Lawyer's Guide to Effective Negotiation and Mediation, CLE edition, is the abridged version of the looseleaf edition designed for use in CLE programs. The section and form numbering from the looseleaf edition have been retained in the CLE edition.

3

process or the means by which terms were created, then even satisfactory settlement terms will leave the party with a negative sense about the process, and perhaps the agreement. A review of the propriety of tactics and strategies need also be included because a lawyer's future success is likely dependent on the reputation that the lawyer builds through prior sessions.

It is difficult to determine which approach to or behavior in a particular negotiation was more effective than some other. The ever-present ethical dimension considers how the results were arrived at by the negotiators, suggesting that "effective" negotiation incorporates appropriate and ethical behavior. A lawyer's duty to provide clients with zealous representation must not be pursued through tactics objectively viewed to be unfair, or which are detrimental to the legitimate concerns of other parties, lawyers, or society at large.

The effective negotiator, then, both maximizes the client's return and maintains a positive and professionally responsible relationship with the "opposition." Theoretically, the concept is simple. In reality, many negotiators get blinded by the possibility of, or worse, opportunity for "cleaning out" the other side. A seemingly wrong move by one negotiator can lead the other negotiator away from propriety and towards new levels of unexpected gain; the latter may produce less than responsible behavior including material untruth, materially false demands or other conduct not penetrable by the recognized tools of negotiation.

§ 2.2 Ethics—A Natural Set of Values

Each participant in a negotiation brings with her to the bargaining table an array of personal and professional ethical beliefs and principles. Roger S. Haydock, *Negotiation Practice* (Wiley Law Publications, 1984) at 195. Religious convictions, personal beliefs, and professional ethics rules or guidelines, (read: requirements) all serve to dictate the extent to which each negotiator will adhere to ethical behavior during a negotiation. *Id.* at 195–199.

To the extent the negotiators find commonality in their approach in terms of shared ethical beliefs, they can proceed to negotiate with some degree of mutual trust. Where the negotiators differ in their perceived moral obligations in the process, there may emerge difficulties exhibited in attitude and behavior. While the perceived ethical obligations among negotiators varies, as a practical matter the ethical character of the negotiators will be reflected in their attitude, manner and behavior.

§ 2.3 Ethics—A Prescribed Set of Values

Lawyers are bound by the code of ethics adopted by their own state and promulgated on models created by the American Bar Association. Every code of ethics is intended to heighten public trust of attorneys through the uniform governance of conduct.

The ABA thirty-two Canons of Ethics ("Canons"), adopted by the ABA in 1908, were subsequently adopted, with some modification, by all but 13 states and the District of Columbia. Difficulties in interpretation and enforcement of the Canons led to the passage in 1969 of the new ABA Code of Professional Conduct ("Code"), eventually adopted by every state except California and Illinois.

The Model Code consists of Ethical Considerations ("ECs") which define aspirational goals and, Disciplinary Rules ("DRs") which set a minimum expectation of behavior for practicing attorneys. The disparity between these two levels of expectation led to the ABA's reconsideration and replacement of the Code in 1983 with the ABA Model Rules of Professional Conduct ("Model Rules") (available on WESTLAW: LS–MRPC database). A majority of states have adopted the Model Rules en toto, or in some variation, while several other states continue to follow the Code.

The provisions of each state's code of ethical conduct govern attorney behavior in negotiating for clients. These obligations as set out in the Model Code and Model Rules include:

A Lawyer's Guide to Effective Negotiation and Mediation, CLE edition, is the abridged version of the looseleaf edition designed for use in CLE programs. The section and form numbering from the looseleaf edition have been retained in the CLE edition.

(1) Providing competent representation of a client. Competent representation requires the legal knowledge, skill, thoroughness and preparation reasonably necessary for the representation. Model Rules of Professional Conduct Rule 1.1.

(2) Representing only those clients which the lawyer has the competency, knowledge and skill to handle. Model Code of Professional Responsibility, DR 6–101.

(3) Acting with reasonable diligence and promptness in representing a client. Model Rules of Professional Conduct Rule 1.3.

(4) Exercising independent professional judgment and rendering candid advice. In rendering advice, a lawyer may refer not only to law, but to other considerations such as moral economic, social and political factors, that may be relevant to the client's situation. Model Rules of Professional Conduct Rule 2.1.

(5) Abiding by a client's decisions concerning the objectives of representation . . . and consulting with the client as to the means by which they are to be pursued. A lawyer shall abide by a client's decision whether to accept an offer of settlement of a matter. . . . Model Rules of Professional Conduct Rule 1.4.

(6) An affirmative obligation to keep the client apprised of matters necessary to the client's making informed decisions in these areas. Model Rules of Professional Conduct Rule 1.2.

In negotiation, then, the lawyer assumes responsibility for technical and legal tactical issues, but defers to the client regarding the ultimate determinations or resolution of the case. Comment, Model Rules of Professional Conduct Rule 1.2 (WESTLAW: LS–MRPC database, **ci(1.2)**).

§ 2.7 Misrepresentation or Lying in Negotiation

Since negotiations are usually conducted between lawyers and sometimes with the presence of the parties, but

A Lawyer's Guide to Effective Negotiation and Mediation, CLE edition, is the abridged version of the looseleaf edition designed for use in CLE programs. The section and form numbering from the looseleaf edition have been retained in the CLE edition.

6

without an intermediary, the participants need to decide for themselves what bits of information will or should be divulged. Underlying the process is the obligation of attorneys to act both as their client's advocate but also as an "officer of the court."

Attorneys representing clients in negotiations are usually justified, at least initially, in not revealing the extent of their settlement authority or the areas of weakness in the case. However, confronted by a direct question on these subjects, an ethical dilemma emerges for the attorney. The lawyer needs to decide, often instantaneously, whether to withhold particular information or to respond candidly, pursuant to the ethical duty to be fair in dealings with other parties.

Some attorneys may believe that lying is "part of the game" and that the use of lies is fair since both sides are aware of it. This position would seem to conflict with a lawyer's duty to uphold an image of good character within the legal profession. Certainly one relevant provision in the Model Code of Professional Responsibility relating to negotiation is DR 1–102(a)(4), which states:

> A lawyer shall not . . . engage in conduct involving dishonesty, fraud, deceit, or misrepresentation.

The failure to specifically reference negotiation in this rule or comments to the rule suggests that this provision was not intended to apply to negotiation proceedings. However, when read in conjunction with the Model Code provision on representing a client within the bounds of the law (DR 7–102(a)(5), the counter-argument emphasizes the Code's focus on honesty and truthful representation. DR 7–102(a)(5) provides:

> In his representation of a client, a lawyer shall not . . . knowingly make a false statement of law or fact.

An attempt to resolve this ethical dilemma in legal negotiations appears in the Model Rules of Professional Conduct which do specifically address negotiation. Model Rule 4.1 (WESTLAW: LS–MRPC database, **ci (4.1)**) states:

A Lawyer's Guide to Effective Negotiation and Mediation, CLE edition, is the abridged version of the looseleaf edition designed for use in CLE programs. The section and form numbering from the looseleaf edition have been retained in the CLE edition.

In the course of representing a client a lawyer shall not knowingly:

(a) make a false statement of material fact or law to a third person; or

(b) fail to disclose a material fact to a third person when disclosure is necessary to avoid assisting a criminal or fraudulent act by a client, unless disclosure is prohibited by Rule 1.6 [on confidentiality of information].

Comment [2] to this Rule clarifies that what constitutes a statement of fact can depend on the circumstances. In addition:

Under generally accepted conventions in negotiation, certain types of statements ordinarily are not taken as statements of material fact. Estimates of price or value placed on the subject of a transaction and a party's intentions as to an acceptable settlement of a claim are in this category, and so is the existence of an undisclosed principal except where nondisclosure of the principal would constitute fraud.

Thus, the Model Rules recognize that lawyers will not tell the whole truth in a negotiation because of the underlying psychological component requiring mutual compromise which accompanies every negotiation.

There remains, however, a fine line between what is impermissible lying and permissible puffing, and between what is an appropriate or inappropriate use of an opponent's weaknesses in crafting a settlement. Harry Edwards and J. White, *The Lawyer as a Negotiator* (West Publishing, 1977) at 372. Although the Model Rules suggest that puffing is permissible and expected, it remains unethical and improper for the lawyer as negotiator to knowingly falsify facts, evidence or legal precedent. *See:* Model Code DR 7–102(a)(5) and (a)(6), Model Rule 3.3(a)(1) (WESTLAW: LS–MRPC database, **ci (3.3)**); Roger S. Haydock, *Negotiation Practice* (Wiley Law Publications, 1984) at 210.

Model Rule 3.4 states that a lawyer shall not:

A Lawyer's Guide to Effective Negotiation and Mediation, CLE edition, is the abridged version of the looseleaf edition designed for use in CLE programs. The section and form numbering from the looseleaf edition have been retained in the CLE edition.

(a) unlawfully obstruct another party's access to evidence or unlawfully alter, destroy or conceal a document or other material having potential evidentiary value. A lawyer shall not counsel or assist another person to do any such act;

(b) falsify evidence, counsel or assist a witness to testify falsely, or offer an inducement to a witness that is prohibited by law.

Thus, there is a great deal of disagreement regarding the extent of disclosure required in a negotiation. *See:* Roger S. Haydock, *Negotiation Practice* (Wiley Law Publications, 1984) at 207–08. Mark K. Schoenfield and R.M. Schoenfield, *Legal Negotiations: Getting Maximum Results* (McGraw–Hill, 1988) at 383. This difficulty in distinction has been well characterized as follows:

> Valid differences of opinion will exist regarding what is a permissible exaggeration, what is an appropriate interpretation, and how likely it is that evidence will be available. Considered differences of opinion will exist regarding what is and what is not a fact. . . . [And] informed differences of opinion may exist justifying the misrepresentation of facts, as long as those facts are not material or relevant to the negotiation. [Thus] these instances reflect borderline situations of proper/improper conduct.

Roger S. Haydock, *Negotiation Practice* (Wiley Law Publications, 1984) at 210.

Attempting to resolve such "borderline situations", under the Model Code, the ABA promulgated several opinions regarding the degree to which misleading is permissible in negotiations. Most notably, in ABA Formal Opinion 314, April 27, 1965 (WESTLAW: LS–ABAEO database, **ci (formal +5 314)**), the ABA stated:

> [W]hat is the duty of a lawyer in regard to disclosure of the weaknesses in his client's case in the course of negotiations for the settlement of a tax case? . . . .
> In the absence of either judicial determination or of a hypothetical exchange of files by adversaries, counsel will always urge in aid of settlement of a controversy

A Lawyer's Guide to Effective Negotiation and Mediation, CLE edition, is the abridged version of the looseleaf edition designed for use in CLE programs. The section and form numbering from the looseleaf edition have been retained in the CLE edition.

Notes

the strong points of his case and minimize the weak. . . . [T]he absolute duty not to make false assertions of fact [does not] require the disclosure of weaknesses in the client's case, and in no event does it require the disclosure of his confidences, unless the facts in the attorney's possession indicate beyond reasonable doubt that a crime will be committed. A wrong, or indeed sometimes an unjust, tax result in the settlement of a controversy is not a crime.

. . .

Prudence may recommend procedures not required by ethical considerations. Thus, even where the lawyer believes that there is no obligation to reflect a transaction in or with his client's return, nevertheless he may, as a tactical matter, advise his client to disclose the transaction in reasonable detail by way of a rider to the return.

The duty to be fair is a duty which each lawyer owes to the profession and to society; it supersedes even the duty owed to the client. Harry Edwards and J. White, *The Lawyer as a Negotiator,* (West Publishing, 1977) at 415. Lawyers will be guided by their own conscience; they should strive to attain the highest level of skill, to improve the law and the legal profession and to exemplify the legal profession's ideals of public service. Model Rules of Professional Conduct, Preamble, [6] (WESTLAW: LS–MRPC database, **ci (preamble)**).

The effective negotiator should not need to resort to lies, fraud or deceit to be persuasive, inventive or successful. Quite to the contrary, the masterful lawyer can be quite successful in negotiation through careful planning, disclosures and phrasing.

§ 2.8 Phrasing to Avoid Deceit

The lawyers' art is their language. Legal training is the study of creating clear meaning (often sacrificed through legalese). Negotiation merely requires the same level of care in language structure as the lawyer brings to drafting documents. Offers and demands should be care-

A Lawyer's Guide to Effective Negotiation and Mediation, CLE edition, is the abridged version of the looseleaf edition designed for use in CLE programs. The section and form numbering from the looseleaf edition have been retained in the CLE edition.

fully constructed to permit flexibility where desired and information can be controlled through language as well.

When making an offer, a sufficient linguistic opening can be made which permits the lawyer to expand the period of consideration. For example, the inflexible: "You have until midnight tonight" is clear, but leaves no room to accept the offer after the stated time. However, modified, the offer becomes: "I'm not sure my client will accept this after midnight tonight" or "I'd have a tough time convincing my client to accept this after midnight tonight" both permit the lawyer ethical means of creating a deadline, but retaining the power to modify.

Similarly, demands can be made flexible: "We will never accept the following . . ." can become "I wouldn't count on us accepting . . ." These simple modifications of language can make the difference between misrepresentation of position and seemingly unmoving, yet ethically flexible, statements of position.

Ethical control over information disclosure can easily be held in the stead of misstatement. It is all too easy to lie. Lawyers need to able to rely on the skills of their craft to insure the presentation of information in an ethical yet strategically controlled manner. Some critics might suggest that if semantics is the difference between right and wrong, then the difference is superficial. This is simply not true. Underlying this criticism is the expectation that most people will hear both negotiation statements (one with flexibility and one without) to be the same thing, i.e., will likely hear the extreme even though the words do not state as such.

The negotiator who is an effective listener *will* hear the difference and be able to respond accordingly. For example, the statement, "I can't see my client accepting an offer after midnight," can be responded to with: "Ah, while unlikely, I am pleased to hear that acceptance is not out of the question after that time." This response may serve to force the challenge and clarify the exact acceptance deadline.

A Lawyer's Guide to Effective Negotiation and Mediation, CLE edition, is the abridged version of the looseleaf edition designed for use in CLE programs. The section and form numbering from the looseleaf edition have been retained in the CLE edition.

§ 2.10 Psychology of Negotiation

Candidly, even noble attempts to create a "win-win" resolution for all parties are unlikely to be successful. In many cases, one negotiator actually obtains more (materially) than the other. The measure of success often lies in the degree to which all parties to the negotiation feel satisfied with the results they have achieved.

Negotiation is a psychological process requiring a give and take between the parties through their lawyers. It is less likely that a negotiator will leave a session satisfied if she has not experienced the give-and-take of the negotiation process with the others. For example, suppose a party desires $5,000.00 to settle. The demand is made for $8,500.00 with the expectation of a reduction to $5,000.00 through the process. However, the recipient of the demand agrees immediately to pay $8,500.00. Is the demanding party happy to have the demand met? In many cases, the answer is no. Why?

The immediate acceptance of an initial offer can trigger the feeling that the initial demand was too small! After all, it was met without dispute so the case must have had a greater value. Objective value aside, it is the avoidance of the psychological process, not the final terms, that creates the satisfaction level. No one wants to believe they have settled on terms which could have been much better. Similarly, imagine the $8,500.00 demand is made to a party who expected to pay $10,000.00. This party now knows they can settle the claim for less than $8,500.00 and will most likely exert effort in that direction regardless of the pre-existing expectation. The negotiators aren't certain whether an error was made by someone in valuation, but they will seize any opportunity to improve their position. It's a psychological need of most people.

Moreover, numbers or terms offered or demanded which are objectively outside of the anticipated range, but nevertheless stated as firm or real, may necessitate a review of the original case valuation. Either a party has somehow misinterpreted some part of the case leading to an inaccurate analysis, or has miscalculated the necessary

---

A Lawyer's Guide to Effective Negotiation and Mediation, CLE edition, is the abridged version of the looseleaf edition designed for use in CLE programs. The section and form numbering from the looseleaf edition have been retained in the CLE edition.

12

terms of an acceptable agreement. A step back needs to be taken to explore the direction of the negotiation and feasibility of creating workable terms.

Negotiation is essentially a competitive exercise in which the lawyer's desire to do well may conflict with the sense of loyalty which the lawyer must always feel for the client. The negotiation must always pursue client interests and the psychological welfare of the client as well. Lawyers should strive to exercise conduct and present a demeanor appropriate to the sanctity of the profession. Failure to do so sets a precedent which can create distrust between the parties or between the parties and their lawyers.

§ 2.14 Keeping the Client Informed and Involved

Clients should be kept abreast of all facets of the settlement negotiation process. The failure to keep a client informed enhances the probability that misunderstandings will result between the attorney and client. In fact, misunderstanding is the single most significant factor which determines whether a case will settle or proceed to trial. Gerald R. Williams, *Legal Negotiation and Settlement* (West Publishing, 1983) at 60.

Lawyers in a study were asked to identify why a case did not settle. Over fifty percent of them blamed their client's unwillingness to accept the settlement figure they had recommended. *Id.* at 59. The obvious question becomes: to what extent did that lawyer review options, considerations and consequences with that client vis-a-vis client goals?

An uninvolved client is likely to become a dissatisfied client; dissatisfaction endangers the success of a negotiation because the client can become angry or disenchanted with the representation afforded by the lawyer. Conversely, lawyers may need to readjust their approach in a negotiation session, sometimes to salvage the relationship with their client. Unfortunately, a change in approach may be at the cost of better settlement terms, had the attorney been able to proceed with her natural manner and with client support.

A Lawyer's Guide to Effective Negotiation and Mediation, CLE edition, is the abridged version of the looseleaf edition designed for use in CLE programs. The section and form numbering from the looseleaf edition have been retained in the CLE edition.

In addition to keeping the client informed on case development, attorneys should create an appropriate level of involvement with their clients; too little contact can create dissatisfaction, but too much contact can also prove to be counterproductive. For example, a client may not understand the importance or routine nature of posturing in the early stages of every negotiation. Moreover, lawyers know that their opponents may need to vent frustration from time to time and that they will present unreasonable positions. The client who is present during these portions of the negotiation sessions is likely to be confused or angered by the interaction.

Clients present and involved in the early stages of a settlement negotiation may decide to accept an offer sensed by the lawyer to be made prematurely in the process. That client might also accidentally or unknowingly disclose important information which hurts their stated position. Mark K. Schoenfield and R.M. Schoenfield, *Legal Negotiations: Getting Maximum Results* (McGraw–Hill, 1988) at 193. See also: Donald G. Gifford, *Legal Negotiation Theory and Applications* (West Publishing, 1989) at 82.

The time to establish the client's understanding of how lawyer contact with that client should proceed and to clarify the lawyer's intention of how contact *will* proceed is during the initial client meeting. Paul M. Lisnek, *Effective Client Communication: A Lawyer's Handbook for Interviewing and Counseling* (West Publishing, 1992), Ch. 4. The lawyer can, at that time, also define when and how the client will participate in settlement discussions.

Clients usually have no understanding of court backlogs, lawyer continuances and heavy lawyer caseloads. Establishing how and when the client can reach the attorney, as well as when the client can expect to hear from the attorney, provides important security that good client relations will be preserved.

Clients should be assured that they will be informed of any offer or request for an offer presented by the other party. This understanding is important for clients so they are prepared for the inevitable periods of inactivity which occur in nearly every case. Paul M. Lisnek, *Effective Client Communication: A Lawyer's Handbook for Interviewing and Counseling* (West Publishing, 1992), § 4.8. Once lawyers have prepared their clients for the importance of their involvement through the case in general, and in settlement negotiations specifically, and after client needs, interests, goals and objectives are established in light of the opposing party's interests and objectives, then lawyers can proceed to explore the best avenue to initiate and undertake settlement negotiations in that case.

Form 2–5, the "Client Contact and Involvement" form assists attorneys in monitoring their contact level with clients. A seemingly simple task, many attorneys do not maintain a sufficient level of contact or interaction with their clients. The form is intended to insure regular contact, but is more likely to be followed only if the lawyer transfers the recorded contact dates specified on the form to a daily diary.

Since many attorneys use some type of daily reminder system, this information transfer may present the most efficient means for insuring that client contact is maintained. Like the due dates for discovery and court appearance dates, client contact dates should be viewed as a fundamental task which cannot be delayed or postponed any easier than it is to get a court continuance. Clients expect the contact and attorneys owe it to them.

§ 2.16 Keys to Effective Negotiation

Every negotiation needs to be preceded by an evaluation of the case and the creation of boundaries for settlement. The keys to a meaningful and ultimately successful negotiation experience are:

(1) Lawyer preparation, including mastery of the facts and law of the case. There is no more important factor than the lawyer's preparation. In essence, preparation incorporates every other factor because the lawyer is not prepared if she does not know client needs, the needs of the other parties, what to disclose and protect, and to communicate the integrated disclosures effectively.

A Lawyer's Guide to Effective Negotiation and Mediation, CLE edition, is the abridged version of the looseleaf edition designed for use in CLE programs. The section and form numbering from the looseleaf edition have been retained in the CLE edition.

Notes

Being unfamiliar with the facts of the case, its areas of strength and weakness, is a certain sign of ultimate failure. Being confronted with case law or local ordinances that impact on one's position, without anticipation, can lead to disastrous concessions and unintended disclosure. Conversely, thorough preparation signals control, composure and confidence; the result is a credible presence and handling of the matter during the negotiations.

(2) Lawyer familiarity with the client's interests and needs.

(3) Lawyer anticipation and evaluation of other parties' needs and interests. Just knowing what one's client seeks in settlement is not sufficient. The lawyer need also be able to reflect her client's needs against the potentially competing or similar needs of the other party or parties. Sometimes, clients will need to adjust their expectations to permit overlap with the other side thereby creating a potential for settlement. The important component here is the anticipation of other interests.

Lawyers should reflect on each need of their client to determine what the corresponding need of the other party will be. This reflection to anticipation process is essential to lawyer planning and analysis. Without it, the lawyer is less able to create a strategy for obtaining the settlement terms necessary to both meet the client's needs and achieve an agreement the client will psychologically find to be satisfying.

(4) Lawyer evaluation of strategy for conducting the negotiation. There is a variety of approaches every lawyer can use in a negotiation; approach may vary with the personalities involved in or circumstances of the negotiation. Lawyers need to reflect upon all of these factors before choosing what approach to take and which techniques to use in the negotiation.

(5) Control over and strategy of information disclosure and protection. Control over disclosure is likely the most common reason for failure in a negotiation which results from the process itself. Unlike the failure to pre-

A Lawyer's Guide to Effective Negotiation and Mediation, CLE edition, is the abridged version of the looseleaf edition designed for use in CLE programs. The section and form numbering from the looseleaf edition have been retained in the CLE edition.

pare, damaging disclosures can be made by the most well prepared of lawyers.

Most lawyers are capable of protecting information specific to their attorney-client relationship; the disclosures referenced here are the non-privileged and therefore technically ethical, but strategically "suicidal" information releases. For example, making reference to a document the negotiator assumes the other side has reviewed, can open up a Pandora's Box of problems. Suppose, for example, the document had not been reviewed due to an incomplete preparation by the other side, the damaging information referred to is now unnecessarily placed onto the table for discussion.

(6) Lawyer understanding of settlement boundaries and limitations. This understanding is often grounded in the understanding of client and other parties' needs, the facts of the case and governing law.

(7) Lawyer communication ability. The simplest factor to state and the one most commonly assumed to be innate. In reality, poor communicative ability is the single most prevalent problem plaguing lawyers. Communication skills are not part of legal training. To the contrary, the study of law brings with it a distance from common meaning and understanding; the result is confusion between lawyer and client which the former often fails to recognize. The solution lies in intentional and directed efforts by lawyers to improve their communication skills, specifically their ability to relate information meaningfully, gather it accurately and create rapport with the client.

§ 2.18 Uncovering the Client's Interests

The real conflict in any negotiation often lies, not in the positions as stated by the parties, but in the psychological distance between the parties' interests and objectives. It is underlying interests which motivate the negotiators through the adjustment and jockeying of positions. If the stated position is the end to be sought, then the interests are what permitted the position to be created.

A Lawyer's Guide to Effective Negotiation and Mediation, CLE edition, is the abridged version of the looseleaf edition designed for use in CLE programs. The section and form numbering from the looseleaf edition have been retained in the CLE edition.

Notes

Attorneys evaluate the desirable direction of the case by reviewing all relevant discovery and law, as they reflect upon the client's interests and needs. The attorney needs to uncover the interests which also lie beneath any stated goals. It is the client's underlying needs and interests which provide the understanding of the motives which drive the objectives. Charles B. Craver, *Effective Legal Negotiation and Settlement* (Michie Company, 1986) at 31–34. These objectives produce goals, or the concrete realities sought in the negotiation.

Uncovering client interests requires the lawyer to gather information from the client. The dialogue exchange should be characterized by open-ended questions which permit clients to relate freely what they need and want in a settlement. The lawyer may ask "Tell me what you hope to get out of this lawsuit?" or "What are you looking for from the other side to settle this case?" or "What is the most important thing you want to achieve when this case is over?" Each of these inquiries permits clients to respond as they wish, with information that should reflect their underlying interests and needs.

The lawyer may need to clarify a client's answer by rephrasing it in terms of need or interest. For example, a client who states: "I want that S.O.B. to pay heavily for what he did," is likely relating feelings of anger and hostility, not clear goals. The lawyer can rephrase the comment to reflect an interest "So, more than a particular dollar amount, you want to insure that your neighbor understands just how angry you are, and how wrong you believe his conduct in this situation is." Grounded in the skill of active listening, the lawyer is better able to uncover the client's needs and interests.

The lawyer needs to reflect interests back to the client accurately; the lawyer may have to modify and clarify what the client says until an accurate identification of needs can be made. The process should not, however, be perceived by the client as patronization. Rather, the lawyer's attempts need to be seen as a sincere effort to help the client understand what is truly being sought and what can be realistically achieved from the negotiation.

A Lawyer's Guide to Effective Negotiation and Mediation, CLE edition, is the abridged version of the looseleaf edition designed for use in CLE programs. The section and form numbering from the looseleaf edition have been retained in the CLE edition.

Throughout the interest identification process, the lawyer needs to keep an ear to what the client does not say. Needs and interests can be overshadowed by emotions, such as frustration or anger. The lawyer should listen to client comments at face value, but then look beneath them for the interests. For example, a demand for a large sum of money can reflect anger, and personal attacks on the other party can reflect hurt or disappointment. Keeping a client on track in an interview clouded by emotion is not an easy task. The lawyer may wish to give the client some time to reflect on what they truly need in the case before continuing to define objectives.

Once the client's needs and interests (bottom line) are clarified, the lawyer next determines how those interests can be transformed into objectives which will drive the creation of goals, or those concrete things to be realized through the negotiation process. The needs and interests need to be carefully couched into objectives, and ultimately into the goals which will be strategically stated as a position by the party in the negotiation.

Objectives are the emotional translation of needs made by the client. Asking clients what they seek from the negotiation may or may not produce a realistic and rational response. The lawyer needs to work carefully with the client in establishing objectives and then creating achievable goals.

§ 2.19 Transforming Client Objectives to Goals

The transformation of objectives to goals often reflects a transition between emotion and reality. A client's objectives are often emotionally based; they seek justice, retribution, security, or peace of mind. These variables need to be reintegrated in terms which are achievable through negotiation.

Justice may translate to limited parental visitation in a custody matter, retribution to money payment, security to interest in property and peace of mind to new work condition provisions in a labor dispute. Essentially, the lawyer needs to help the client define what concrete

A Lawyer's Guide to Effective Negotiation and Mediation, CLE edition, is the abridged version of the looseleaf edition designed for use in CLE programs. The section and form numbering from the looseleaf edition have been retained in the CLE edition.

Notes

things are the representation of the less concrete objectives. The translation produces goals.

Conversely, some clients know specifically what they want out of a negotiation ("A million dollars!" "Everything she's got!"), which may or may not be based in reality. In these instances, the lawyer evaluates the stated goals in terms of their underlying objectives. If the goals are unrealistic based on the case circumstances (a million dollar demand in a minor personal injury matter, for example), then the lawyer may need to explore the underlying objectives to see whether the client is willing to modify their negotiation goals accordingly.

In many cases, clients can be made to see the need for adjusting their expectations. For example, a family who loses a child in an automobile accident may be strongly resistant to accepting a $50,000.00 insurance policy limit offer. "Our child is worth more!" Through counseling and evaluation with the lawyer, the family may come to realize that no dollar figure will ever compensate the loss; their grief is clouding the reality of settlement potential. Perhaps a public trial is their only means to realize acceptance.

§ 2.20 An Eye to the Other Party

The lawyer's interaction with the client should be conducted with an eye towards the opposing party's anticipated response to demands or offers made. In addition, consideration need be given to the other party's needs and interests (bottom line), objectives and goals. This reflection should create the ability to determine the appropriateness, potential outcome and consequences of each demand, offer or concession made. Each such position need be measured against the client's bottom line needs and upper level goals.

This extensive preparation and analysis are components of every lawyer and client's desire to minimize the potential for loss. Preparation permits a determination of the break-even point (materially and psychologically) and levels of realized reward.

A Lawyer's Guide to Effective Negotiation and Mediation, CLE edition, is the abridged version of the looseleaf edition designed for use in CLE programs. The section and form numbering from the looseleaf edition have been retained in the CLE edition.

The process of identifying and understanding possible outcomes is assisted through the technique of brainstorming. This technique is useful in identification, a process that precedes evaluation or analysis and which must not incorporate evaluation or judgment at the beginning of the information generating stage.

§ 2.23 Creation of Position

Once the outcome continuum is completed, the client and attorney are better able to discuss the goals and positioning for the negotiation. They can define the nature and extent of concessions that can be made in the negotiation. This process should be undertaken with an understanding of the negotiation's "integrative potential."

Integrative potential is the extent to which the parties can reach an agreement to each of their satisfactions. During the creation of position, the lawyer should expect clients to have high expectations for settlement. To a client, a goal is simply an objective made concrete, which can reflect an inability to see obstacles or a need to make any concession.

Focus needs to be placed by the lawyer on the outcome continuum as the monitor of reality; each request or demand by one party is likely to be met by one of equal and potentially opposite proportion by the other side. Once the client comes to understand the relationship between possible settlement outcomes and his own needs, he is more likely to construct a realistic expectation about the negotiation.

These preliminary steps should not be avoided. To the contrary, this process creates or confirms a sense of reality in the client regarding the negotiation position to be taken. Often, clients send their lawyers off to negotiate with a set of unreasonable or unobtainable goals, only to be disappointed when the negotiation breaks down. The attorney-client relationship can experience substantial harm if the client lacks a sense of realism about the negotiation process and the attorney cannot instill such a sense. A negotiation position needs to be based on realis-

A Lawyer's Guide to Effective Negotiation and Mediation, CLE edition, is the abridged version of the looseleaf edition designed for use in CLE programs. The section and form numbering from the looseleaf edition have been retained in the CLE edition.

tic expectations, while simultaneously meeting the needs and underlying interests of the client.

Form 2–12 is the "Negotiation Position" Form. Once the lawyer has established a set of realistic goals based on manageable objectives, she can work with the client to establish the boundaries of the position. Seeking more than is needed, and clarifying what may be conceded, the negotiation position is drafted jointly by lawyer and client. This becomes the beginning guideline for the negotiation. Both lawyer and client should anticipate modifying their position upon a consideration of the other party's expected needs and goals.

§ 2.24 Determining the Needs, Objectives and Goals of the Other Side

Negotiating would be a simple exercise indeed if there was no one taking an opposing or adversarial position. Unfortunately, there is always another party who comes to the negotiation with their own set of needs, objectives and goals. Moreover, the other side is just as interested in and committed to its own position.

Thus, the attorney and client should discuss not only their own needs, interests, goals and objectives for the negotiation, but those of the other side as well. It is often difficult to anticipate what the opponent's underlying objectives and interests are without substantial history with that person. Prior interaction provides information as to how that person thinks and what they might be after in a settlement. The client can assist in this regard, assuming the client has and can relate the interactional history with the other party to the lawyer.

Without the insight of prior interactions with the other side to the negotiation, it is nearly impossible to determine the position that the adversary will take in the negotiation session. The effective negotiator need be sensitive during the negotiation to the opponent's needs and goals as they are stated or suggested through commentary or conduct. Only with this foundation of information can an evaluation be made of the potential for an integrated solution. Even if the potential for overlap in inter-

A Lawyer's Guide to Effective Negotiation and Mediation, CLE edition, is the abridged version of the looseleaf edition designed for use in CLE programs. The section and form numbering from the looseleaf edition have been retained in the CLE edition.

22

ests is low, the lawyers will nevertheless seek to achieve as much as possible for their clients.

The lawyer and client can begin to define the interests of the other side by reviewing their own needs, interests, objectives and goals; some of the other party's needs may be similar while others may be mirror opposites of the other's. Anticipating the needs of an adversarial party includes considering the interests, which would underlie any particular need. Once determining needs based on interests, underlying emotional objectives may be revealed from which the goals will emerge.

The purpose for identifying the other side's interests and needs should be clear enough:

(1) It is easier to control interaction with a knowledge of what the other side needs or wants;

(2) The likelihood of resolution is greater if the needs of the other party can be met;

(3) The likelihood of meeting one's own needs may be improved by knowing what and how to create an offer to the other side; and

(4) Interaction dynamics, including reactions, can be better anticipated and guided, thus creating better control.

Thorough research and investigation are integral to preparation. All relevant law must be reviewed and everything learned through discovery needs to be considered and reflected upon with regard to the settlement position. The goals and objectives established with the client may not be realistic in the face of law which limits recovery, or discovery which fails to support the position.

In many cases, settlement negotiations are not entered into until sufficient discovery has been completed. Thus, lawyers who have initial familiarity with their clients' needs and goals can work to gather the necessary supporting information through remaining discovery. Relevant documents not previously disclosed may need to be requested, facts useful to have confirmed may be established through a request to admit and other information

A Lawyer's Guide to Effective Negotiation and Mediation, CLE edition, is the abridged version of the looseleaf edition designed for use in CLE programs. The section and form numbering from the looseleaf edition have been retained in the CLE edition.

§ 2.24

Notes

can be explored through deposition. Each component of discovery becomes a tool to be shared with the client in preparation for the negotiation.

Lawyers should utilize the vast arsenal of information they gather and evaluate. If the negotiation needs to be postponed until additional information can be gathered, then it is worth the delay which permits the strengthening of one's position. For example, some cases may necessitate the consultation of an expert as an important part of preparation.

Form 2–14, the Lawyer Negotiation Preparation Form, sets out the consideration of governing laws and case discovery. The temptation to begin negotiating without thorough preparation, but just to dig into the meat of the matter is appealing. However, the significant possibility of making an agreement that falls short of the client's needs and interests should strongly establish the importance of making use of this form. Once lawyers complete all preparation for the negotiation with the input of the client, they can turn to the issues of how and when to conduct the process. Clearly, the atmosphere and conditions of negotiation will impact the process and ultimately shape the nature or terms of the agreement.

A Lawyer's Guide to Effective Negotiation and Mediation, CLE edition, is the abridged version of the looseleaf edition designed for use in CLE programs. The section and form numbering from the looseleaf edition have been retained in the CLE edition.

Form 2–1

Valuing a Case

Case Name _____

File No. _____

Attorney _____

Factors	Initial Estimate	Revisions: —investigation —discovery —negotiation
A. Actual Costs:		
1. Medical		
2. Actual Lost		
Earnings		
3a. Property		
Damage		
3b. Replacement/		
Repair Costs		
4. Other Actual		
Costs (specify)		
B. Other Damages:		
1a. Future Medical		
1b. Pain and		
Suffering		
2. Future Lost		
Earnings		
3. Punitive Damages		
(appropriate?—		
specify reasoning)		
4. Other		

*

Form 2–12

Negotiation Position

Case Name _____

File No. _____

Attorney _____

1. Reevaluate client's needs and interests:

    —Review Form 2–8—

Notes:

2. Reevaluate client's objectives and goals:

    —Review Form 2–9—

Notes:

3. Consider options from the option continuum (Form 2–11) and select and rank the most favorable (overall position outcome for client):

1.

2.

3.

4.

5.

4. Transform options into positions:

    Consider for each selected option what the boundaries of the resulting position would be and what could be conceded:

Position	Boundaries (what cannot be conceded)	What could be conceded
1.		
2.		
3.		
4.		
5.		

Notes:

*

Form 2–12

Form 2–14

Lawyer Negotiation Preparation Form

Case Name _____

File No. _____

Attorney _____

1. Relevant legal considerations:

    A. Statutory:

    B. Caselaw:

2. Facts gained through discovery:

Fact: How gained   Confirmed?
                           (Interrogatory, Request to
                           produce documents, Re-
                           quest to admit)

3. Discovery applications:

    A. Information still needed to support negotiation position:

Information Needed: How to Be Obtained:

    B. Information to resist disclosure in negotiation if possible:

Fact: Why necessary to   Consequences of disclosure
                           restrain disclosure

Notes:

29   Form 2–14

Chapter 3

ESTABLISHING PROPER NEGOTIATING CONDITIONS

Table of Sections

WESTLAW Electronic Research

See WESTLAW Electronic Research Guide preceding the Summary of Contents.

Notes

§ 3.1 Selecting the Negotiation Mechanism

Once a lawyer receives an offer or demand in a case, he is likely to plunge head-first into negotiation, whether responding to the offer by picking up the telephone, by drafting a response, or by setting up a meeting. In all cases, the process quickly blossoms and the negotiators shift right to the heart of the matter. In most cases, too quick a response is a mistake.

Chapter Two emphasized the importance of thorough planning, with significant time spent drafting a negotiation plan. Avoiding or otherwise failing to properly prepare for a negotiation enhances the possibility of a negotiation which will end with terms that are less desirable than had been hoped for by the lawyer and client.

There are two reasons for this consequence:

(1) the negotiator does not have the complete set of facts and accompanying analysis at hand; and (2) the negotiator has not considered the best channel or means for conducting the negotiation. Deciding how to conduct the negotiation is a decision as important as the other preparatory considerations which are made prior to beginning any discussions with the other parties.

A Lawyer's Guide to Effective Negotiation and Mediation, CLE edition, is the abridged version of the looseleaf edition designed for use in CLE programs. The section and form numbering from the looseleaf edition have been retained in the CLE edition.

Notes

The negotiation process can be far more successful when consideration is given by the negotiators to the best mechanism for negotiating and to the atmosphere in which the process will be best conducted. These preliminary environmental considerations include the likelihood for interruptions, the extent of unpleasant climatic conditions, the availability or lack of amenities, and noise. Larry L. Teply, *Legal Negotiation in a Nutshell* (West Publishing, 1991) at 136.

Of course, there are some negotiators who handle themselves quite well spontaneously; others need to take time to reflect on the time, place and manner in which the negotiation will occur. Given the option, it is best for all negotiators to consider these issues to insure they are not taken off guard by circumstances.

Unless an immediate deadline is placed on the decision time, there is little reason for a lawyer in receipt of a demand or offer *not* to take time to reflect and consider the best way to respond. There may be times that immediate contact is invaluable, and other times when some distance created through the delay of a written response is the better alternative.

For example, one negotiator might want to grab at an excellent offer while another might want to let some time pass hoping that even more can be gained. While the latter negotiator might gain more through the process, she might also lose what was previously offered because it is withdrawn before it is accepted. Such is the risk created through delay, whether intentional or not.

Once a negotiation is to take place, the time, place and manner of negotiating are *not* inconsequential to the process. To the contrary, these factors can determine the direction and outcome of the negotiation itself. Whether to meet in one negotiator's office, or the other's, or whether the negotiation occurs in a seemingly neutral location is a choice to be made carefully.

Is interruption desirable? Is privacy essential? How available to office staff will the negotiator be if discussion is pursued on neutral turf? These considerations are important depending on the complexity and sensitivity levels of the matters to be discussed.

In addition, the determination of negotiation atmosphere or setting will vary with the personality of the negotiators. An opponent of objectively lesser negotiation skill may be better controlled by an opponent in face-to-face interaction, while an opponent of greater skill may better be handled through written offers and demands which provide more time for planning and execution. How one calculates the negotiation abilities of the other side is not an easy task. Only that other person's reputation or previous negotiation history provides a sense of how skilled an opponent is being confronted.

Is the person adversarial? Cordial? Prepared? These considerations provide valuable insight which can help determine whether an in-person meeting is the most beneficial for the particular case.

Certainly one means of uncovering such information is to contact colleagues who have experience with the other negotiator and who can report back on that person's style and tactics. It is important to remember that even this historical information will be tainted by two factors: (1) the personality of the reporting negotiator who certainly played a role in setting the dynamics and atmosphere reported, and (2) case specific components that may have guided the previous interaction. Thus, a negotiator seeking information about another negotiator should include in the inquiry some details about the previous case and consider the extent to which the personality of the reporting negotiator guided the process.

The pressures of negotiation can be great indeed; thus, the time used to reflect upon the most desirable setting and conditions in which to discuss settlement is most important. Assuming that few negotiators actually take the time to establish the most beneficial setting for interaction, it seems appropriate to conclude that those negotiators who do take the requisite time to create a desirable atmosphere will have a greater sense of aware-

A Lawyer's Guide to Effective Negotiation and Mediation, CLE edition, is the abridged version of the looseleaf edition designed for use in CLE programs. The section and form numbering from the looseleaf edition have been retained in the CLE edition.

ness over the process. This psychological advantage can prove to be controlling as the negotiation proceeds.

There are three mechanisms by which settlement negotiations can be conducted: over the telephone, in writing, or face-to-face. There are advantages and disadvantages to each of these choices, all of which need to be considered prior to the selection of the medium in any specific case. Once the negotiation mechanism (telephone, in-person or writing) is selected, the negotiators need agree to the timing of and participants in the negotiation. In the case of in-person negotiation, the negotiators need to decide upon the location, setting and atmosphere in which the discussion will be held.

§ 3.2   Telephone Negotiation—In General

The greater majority of settlement discussions take place over the telephone. It is apparent that telephone discussions are, by definition, less personal than a face-to-face meeting. The absence of nonverbal cues on the telephone (with the exception of voice cues) and the meaning which accompanies them effects the dynamics of the communication.

Telephone conversations screen out the myriad of nonverbal cues (eye contact, facial expressions, dress and body gestures) which accompany the verbal message. For this reason, many people avoid face-to-face contact for the comparatively greater degree of comfort and control provided by other mechanisms, such as the telephone. For example, a relatively young or inexperienced lawyer could be intimidated by aggressive or negative facial or bodily cues exhibited by the adversary negotiator.

The resulting feelings in the less experienced negotiator may cause a sense of discomfort, with the result that he may then have difficulty maintaining composure in the process. On the telephone, all of the facial and bodily cues are eliminated as tactics; the age and experience differentials become less relevant in the process. Some negotiators will seek to gain control in telephone conversations through verbal inquiries about past cases creating a sense of discomfort in the absence of most nonverbal cues.

A Lawyer's Guide to Effective Negotiation and Mediation, CLE edition, is the abridged version of the looseleaf edition designed for use in CLE programs. The section and form numbering from the looseleaf edition have been retained in the CLE edition.

Thus, efforts to create intimidation grounded in the difference in experience level can be triggered in telephone negotiations only by asking a series of questions that explore this point. This effort to create intimidation can be countered with an appropriate response such as, "Why don't we just focus on the case at hand. My past experience doesn't much matter here as we both have clients to represent . . ." It is important that a response of this sort is given or the experienced negotiator will create a disparity in effectiveness and ability that can be unnerving.

Substantively, telephone negotiations can be as dispositive as in-person negotiation. Both settings require immediacy in response, although the latter carries many more nonverbal cues. Regardless, it is important for lawyers to prepare for a telephone negotiation in the same way as they might prepare for an in-person meeting.

Put differently, negotiating technique and strategy for a telephone session should be selected with the same careful consideration of the face-to-face meeting because the exchange is immediate, spontaneous and committing. In a general sense, negotiators should discuss important matters in person, not over the telephone; the latter makes it too easy to terminate the discussion by hanging up the telephone. Larry L. Teply, *Legal Negotiation in a Nutshell* (West Publishing, 1991) at 143.

Mistakes in disclosure are likely to be made over the telephone just as they are face-to-face. Only the written medium provides sufficient time for careful construction and presentation of an initial or responsive position. Conversely, a quick thinking and articulate negotiator will evaluate what is said and relate an appropriate response without the lengthy time afforded by written negotiations. As such, there are a variety of reasons to pursue the immediate interactive mechanism of the telephone.

There are several advantages to conducting negotiations over the telephone:

(1) Fewer interaction-based distractions exist in a telephone conversation which could interfere with the busi-

A Lawyer's Guide to Effective Negotiation and Mediation, CLE edition, is the abridged version of the looseleaf edition designed for use in CLE programs. The section and form numbering from the looseleaf edition have been retained in the CLE edition.

35

ness at hand. These include facial expressions, body movement, spacial control and appearance.

(2) Vocal cues are more readily discernible over the telephone than in person. For example, it is often easier to detect deception through leakage in the voice when heard over the telephone than when it is listened to in person.

(3) There are fewer competing cues which permit a focus on the meaning of words and vocal accompaniment. Lawyers can terminate a telephone discussion more easily than they can leave an in-person meeting. The benefit becomes clear when more information or time is needed to think about or consider a proposal.

(4) Notes can be kept at hand, left open and consulted more readily than if the discussion was conducted in the presence of the other party. There is no fear of the other side seeing a protected document.

(5) A telephone call is often less stressful than an in-person meeting since business can be gotten to and through more expediently. In-person meetings often entail more orientation and positioning.

(6) It is easier to say "No" to the other party over the telephone than it is in-person. In fact, it is all too easy to hang up the telephone when the conversation is not going as hoped. Where a negotiator wishes, she can persist in efforts to produce a concession or an agreement with a specific term by rejecting any other suggested terms.

(7) The caller has the advantage of being better prepared to discuss settlement terms than the receiver of the call, if the latter has not reviewed the file prior to the call. In such case, the recipient may wish to exercise advantage (3) above by requesting more time to review the file.

The lawyer can offer to return the call at a later time providing the receiving negotiator with a psychological advantage of preparation upon returning the call. To avoid any such advantage, the parties can agree to a time certain when the discussions will be held, and who will initiate the conference.

A Lawyer's Guide to Effective Negotiation and Mediation, CLE edition, is the abridged version of the looseleaf edition designed for use in CLE programs. The section and form numbering from the looseleaf edition have been retained in the CLE edition.

There are a number of disadvantages to using the telephone as the medium for negotiating.

(1) Telephone conversations tend to be more abbreviated than in-person conversations, thereby providing less assurance that all information and positions have been thoroughly explored and considered.

(2) The telephone is less revealing than personal interaction of the demeanor and intent of the other negotiator. While one lawyer may enjoy the control over her own cues, there is also great value in having the insight into the demeanor and intent of the other negotiator provided by these in-person cues.

(3) Either negotiator can terminate the telephone conversation easily. Thus, neither person has much control over the duration of the negotiation session, requiring each negotiator to exert effort to present a cooperative telephone demeanor.

(4) Since the receiver of a call may choose to say she is not available to negotiate at that time and will need to reschedule the call, the caller's advantage can be disarmed. A negotiator is better advised to state she is too busy to talk, at the time, than to admit that she is unprepared. An impression created that one is unprepared can carry over into future negotiation sessions making the establishment of credibility a requirement that could have been avoided.

§ 3.3 Negotiating in Writing

Lawyers spend much of their time writing briefs, motions and letters. It is interesting that more legal negotiation is not conducted through written dialogue. Some lawyers prefer the break from writing in negotiation to get a better reading of the intent and real objectives of the other side; others forsake the pursuit of insight for the clarity of thought a written offer permits. The written word is more difficult to challenge and carries a longer reach as letters or memoranda can be distributed and shared between all concerned.

A Lawyer's Guide to Effective Negotiation and Mediation, CLE edition, is the abridged version of the looseleaf edition designed for use in CLE programs. The section and form numbering from the looseleaf edition have been retained in the CLE edition.

Notes

There are several advantages to conducting negotiation in writing.

(1) Misunderstandings can be more easily avoided. The drafter has the time and opportunity to set out the settlement position or terms of agreement, sentences can be carefully structured, terms can be qualified and requirements made unequivocal.

(2) The recipient of a written proposal has the requisite time to review terms and modify their substance or manner of presentation. Input can be gotten from colleagues as well. It is most difficult to obtain this type of advice or counsel in anything other than a written negotiation.

Even where time is granted to one negotiator by another for the consideration of an oral proposal, it is difficult to obtain advice that will include sufficient insight on negotiator presentation style and tactic; advice for written proposals can be more clearly focused and guided as the response is drafted.

(3) The task can be handled without interruption. Even if there is disturbance during the preparation, the final draft will flow clearly and directly as the writer chooses. As indicated in advantage (2), it can also be reviewed for accuracy and strategy by others.

(4) The written offer or demand is presented without interruption. The recipient will most likely read the terms in their entirety, thus avoiding the frustration of interruption if the same terms were to be presented in person or over the telephone.

The advantages to written negotiations should be considered in light of the disadvantages which mark a negotiation in writing:

(1) Since a recipient reader is provided an opportunity to study the written offer or demand, a response can be planned just as carefully by the other negotiator. Conversely, oral negotiation can lead to spontaneous concessions or other favorable commentary which can be used to better one's position, a possibility not usually permitted in written negotiation.

(2) Written negotiation is a far slower medium than in-person or telephone interaction. Delay can be a detriment when time is of the essence to the situation. Some deals can be missed or passed upon, or a settlement lost, simply because there was too much time provided to the other negotiator to reflect.

(3) The lawyer time expended to draft written negotiation documents is far more extensive than is a telephone or in-person meeting. The results are larger legal fees and case delays.

The decision to use or not use written negotiation should consider the ability of the negotiator to think on her feet, the importance of time to the process in the specific case and the need for careful control of terms at every step. Certainly, even verbal negotiations will eventually be reduced to writing which will need to clarify the terms agreed to by the negotiators.

§ 3.4   In–Person Negotiation—Location

Some negotiators believe that the strategy of negotiation begins in the moments which follow the exchange of greetings between the negotiators. In reality, planning begins well before the negotiation ever commences and includes consideration of the location in which the settlement discussions will be conducted. Negotiations are affected by their surrounding environment and existing atmosphere; this preliminary matter should not be considered lightly or dismissed as a matter of course.

In-person negotiation can take place at a number of different locations: the office of a party or lawyer, another place selected by one of those people, or at a mutually selected neutral location, such as a restaurant, hotel, or meeting hall. A truly neutral location is one where neither negotiator is a regular who knows the staff or has free access. Neutrality sets the negotiators at an even level for discussion. Selecting the meeting place for conducting a negotiation, a seemingly non-essential task, raises a variety of considerations.

A Lawyer's Guide to Effective Negotiation and Mediation, CLE edition, is the abridged version of the looseleaf edition designed for use in CLE programs. The section and form numbering from the looseleaf edition have been retained in the CLE edition.

Lisnek Effective Negotiation & Mediation—3
CLE Edition

39

Notes

There are several advantages to hosting the negotiation at one's own office:

(1) There is ready access to approval of terms, supervisors, records, documents, or other needed materials.

(2) There is an ability to control the atmosphere and timetable of the negotiation through the setting of the room in which the interaction will occur. The setting can be made comfortable or uncomfortable, the choice of which will affect the tone of the interaction. See § 3.5, *infra*.

(3) Arrangements can be made to get "called away" to attend to "other matters" if desired or needed during the negotiation. Such breaks can be essential to relieve tension or permit consideration by both or all sides.

(4) There is a psychological advantage to being at home. These include familiarity with the atmosphere and a higher comfort level with those surroundings relative to other parties.

(5) It is less expensive in terms of travel and time to host the negotiation meeting. Others need to expend greater time and potential expense to reach the location.

While it may be advantageous to host the negotiation, there are also some benefits to conducting settlement negotiations at the opponent's office. These include:

(1) There are fewer distractions from the task at hand by one's own office staff, unless they are able to reach the negotiation via the telephone or beeper; availability remains the option of the negotiator.

(2) There is better control and protection over the disclosure of information not requested by the hosting person to be brought to the negotiation. Certainly, documents necessary to the discussion or to a resolution of the matter should not intentionally be withheld; intentional attempts to thwart sincere negotiation are unethical. However, there is no obligation to assist an opponent who failed to prepare thoroughly for the session by providing documents or information not appropriately requested.

A Lawyer's Guide to Effective Negotiation and Mediation, CLE edition, is the abridged version of the looseleaf edition designed for use in CLE programs. The section and form numbering from the looseleaf edition have been retained in the CLE edition.

(3) The hosting party can be requested to meet with superiors, who are likely accessible, regarding authority or to seek clarification of issues. This is a significant control element since many negotiators claim that they do not possess sufficient authority to agree to specific terms. Not to comply would appear to be bad faith negotiation so the likelihood is that the negotiator will talk to a person of authority when requested to do so.

(4) The host of the negotiation may sense or be perceived to have a burden to begin the negotiation session by setting out the initial terms of a settlement. If she does so, the host may be providing useful information to the other negotiator. Since information is power, the disclosure may also provide a degree of control to the other side.

Parties sensitive to maintaining a balance of power in negotiation will often agree to meet in a location other than one of the lawyers' or parties' offices. A mutually favorite restaurant or hotel is an appealing option. However, the parties should be careful to avoid a location where either party is a "regular" at or otherwise has significant knowledge of the location. In instances of such familiarity, the advantages of control associated with home office are triggered again.

A neutral location for negotiating may appear to be the most favorable for its seeming sense of equality. Such is only true if neither negotiator has a history at the location (i.e. one negotiator's favorite restaurant). If a neutral location is selected, the negotiators should insure that the location has:

(1) A telephone available for use should it become necessary to secure additional authority.

(2) A private room or seating area to insure that the discussions are not overheard by anyone. Disclosures heard by others could lead to a conflict of interest if the person who overhears happens to be a lawyer who is involved in a related case. As a rule, sensitive information needs to be protected at all cost.

A Lawyer's Guide to Effective Negotiation and Mediation, CLE edition, is the abridged version of the looseleaf edition designed for use in CLE programs. The section and form numbering from the looseleaf edition have been retained in the CLE edition.

(3) Sufficient operating hours to insure the negotiations may continue without interruption. Nothing can be as disconcerting to a negotiation as nearing an agreement, but having to adjourn the proceedings because the location is closing.

(4) Paper and other supplies available should they be needed in the session. Obviously, there is little problem when the negotiation occurs in an office, but this may be of concern when the negotiators meet in a neutral location.

(5) No distractions, such as kitchen or other noises which can disturb the concentration necessary to progress effectively through the negotiations. Locations with background noises that add to the pleasure of a social meeting can be extremely disturbing when concentration becomes a key component.

§ 3.6 Timing as a Negotiation Tool

The timing of a negotiation is important in terms of: (1) the stage of development of the case, and (2) the available negotiation time for the session. In other words, a case needs to be ripe for settlement discussion and the negotiators need to have sufficient time available to handle all the issues that arise. Either or both of these timing factors can have a dramatic impact on the nature of the interaction and the results of the negotiation.

Some negotiations are uncomfortably hurried along by negotiators who claim to have deadline pressures or other conflicts which require the session to end. The expression of such anxiety places that negotiator in a position of less control since the opponent can respond, "That's too bad for us and our clients; I have all the time in the world to discuss the issues."

A negotiation that begins early in the day permits the parties a significant period of time to discuss the matter. Conversely, negotiations begun late in the day create pressure on the negotiators to move quickly towards settlement or deadlock, without the benefit of thoughtful analysis.

A Lawyer's Guide to Effective Negotiation and Mediation, CLE edition, is the abridged version of the looseleaf edition designed for use in CLE programs. The section and form numbering from the looseleaf edition have been retained in the CLE edition.

A competitive lawyer may claim to be unavailable to negotiate or say that another meeting awaits her. Another seemingly cooperative lawyer may claim that he has made efforts to contact the other side, while subsequent investigation shows the attempts were made during the lunch hour or after 6:00 p.m. Using time as a tactic can frustrate the recipient who seeks resolution.

Negotiators are best advised to establish an agreed upon time for their meeting. If one negotiator violates the agreement without explanation, the recipient should clarify with immediacy, that such attempts to control the interaction will not be tolerated in the future. Charles B. Craver, *Effective Legal Negotiation and Settlement* (Michie Company, 1986) at 53.

Put differently, a negotiator can only get away with control tactics that the other negotiators permit. Violations of expectation that go unaddressed serve to create a norm that rules are merely suggestive. The danger in such a norm of noncompliance is that commitment to position can be sidestepped as well. Negotiators need to be consistent in their reactions to violations of expectations.

While clients often want their lawyers to pursue settlements diligently and early in a case, the lawyers should consider whether the case is ripe for settlement. If discovery is not completed, the lawyer should consider the extent to which initiating discussions would be fruitful; an opposing party willing to discuss settlement before there is compliance with an outstanding production request may concede more than is necessary in the case, or may fail to demand sufficient terms for an equitable settlement.

The ripeness of a case suggests that negotiation can be initiated too early for one party or all parties to proceed with sufficient knowledge to negotiate effectively. For example, it may be to one party's advantage to postpone initiating negotiation until well after discovery has begun in a case.

Suppose a complaining party's damages are continuing and require that additional information be obtained through discovery. Such a situation would support a need

A Lawyer's Guide to Effective Negotiation and Mediation, CLE edition, is the abridged version of the looseleaf edition designed for use in CLE programs. The section and form numbering from the looseleaf edition have been retained in the CLE edition.

43

to delay settlement discussions until the negotiators could obtain and review the necessary information. Parties need to weigh the likelihood that a favorable result can be reached before trial and before available monies or other negotiation resources are exhausted.

The manipulation of time by a negotiator is but one variable used to create, measure and reflect power. Perhaps one defendant wishes to conduct settlement discussions prior to the release of a report that would establish its liability. A carefully listening plaintiff might wish to wait until discovery proceeds, suspecting that there may be position strengthening information yet to come.

A Lawyer's Guide to Effective Negotiation and Mediation, CLE edition, is the abridged version of the looseleaf edition designed for use in CLE programs. The section and form numbering from the looseleaf edition have been retained in the CLE edition.

PART II

CONDUCTING THE NEGOTIATION

Chapter 4

STYLES OF NEGOTIATION

Table of Sections

WESTLAW Electronic Research

See WESTLAW Electronic Research Guide preceding the Summary of Contents.

Notes

§ 4.2   The Competitive Negotiator

The negotiator who views negotiation as a competitive process, i.e., has a competitive style of negotiation, believes the parties to a negotiation to be in competition. The negotiation itself is viewed by the competitive negotiator as an adversarial proceeding. Regardless of the techniques employed or cordial, seemingly cooperative, approach taken in the negotiation, the competitive negotiator always seeks to obtain everything possible for the client. In reality, competitive negotiators are not concerned with meeting the needs of the other negotiator or party, although they may appear to be concerned.

From an emotional or psychological perspective, the intimidating nature of the competitive negotiator is focused on the emotional issues of the case. They sidestep the objective merits of the case in favor of a focus on their opponents' emotions and stability. The effective competitive negotiator's goal is to deal with an opponent who has lost confidence in his person and position, who has re-

---

A Lawyer's Guide to Effective Negotiation and Mediation, CLE edition, is the abridged version of the looseleaf edition designed for use in CLE programs. The section and form numbering from the looseleaf edition have been retained in the CLE edition.

45

duced his expectations on what can be accomplished in the case and is prepared to accept less than he otherwise would in a settlement agreement. Larry L. Teply, *Legal Negotiation in a Nutshell* (West Publishing, 1991) at 95.

A cordial approach by competitive negotiators can become a deterrent to effective bargaining because these negotiators fail to press their opponents on crucial issues or interests; they simply seek their own interests. Essentially, regardless of presented demeanor, the relationship between negotiators is not viewed as a cooperative effort for mutual gain by a competitive negotiator.

Competitive negotiators psychologically view every opponent as an adversary. A competitive negotiator enters into each negotiation with a high aspiration level of what he plans to obtain through the process. Competitive negotiators make high demands initially and continue to do so throughout the negotiation; they avoid making concessions if at all possible, and any concessions a competitive negotiator makes are often small. The general sense of a competitive negotiator is that concession means weakness. This presents an interesting contrast with the cooperative negotiator who fundamentally views concession as a sign of mutual interest. How can resolution ever be achieved if all negotiators do not work together to meet the mutual needs of all parties? The competitive negotiator has the response: he is not concerned with the needs or interests of anyone but his own client.

The underlying purpose of a competitive negotiator is to utilize techniques and strategies which are directed *against* the other person in word and action, rather than in accord with that person's interests. The competitive negotiator may use competitive tactics of exaggeration, ridicule, threat, bluff and accusation in order to create a high level of tension in the negotiation and put pressure on the opponent. Larry L. Teply, *Legal Negotiation in a Nutshell* (West Publishing, 1991) at 95. However, competitive negotiators familiar with negotiation theory may disguise their orientation and style by intentionally appearing cooperative and pretending to be concerned about the opponent's needs.

A Lawyer's Guide to Effective Negotiation and Mediation, CLE edition, is the abridged version of the looseleaf edition designed for use in CLE programs. The section and form numbering from the looseleaf edition have been retained in the CLE edition.

In reality, the knowing competitive negotiator uses cooperative techniques with an eye towards personal accomplishment and not the interests of the other side; the goal may be to lull the opponent into concession through the appearance of cooperation. Research on negotiator style would be hesitant to support this approach; a cooperative acts cooperatively and a competitive acts competitively. In reality, the sophisticated negotiator comes to know the tactics and techniques of all other negotiators and can adapt to meet the situation. It would certainly be more characteristic of the competitive negotiator to take the lead by appearing cooperative.

The competitive negotiator should not be seen in terms of good or bad, or right and wrong. Rather, the evaluation should be made in terms of the effectiveness of the negotiator. There are negotiators who can make the style work for the advantage of themselves and their clients, and there are others who turn others off in the process, leading to no resolution and a termination of the efforts.

The effective competitive negotiator can be characterized as tough, dominating, and aggressive. These negotiators enter a negotiation with three essential objectives: (1) a desire for maximum settlement for the client; (2) the desire for the best possible fee for themselves; and (3) a desire to be more strategic than their opponents. Larry L. Teply, *Legal Negotiation in a Nutshell* (West Publishing, 1991) at 96.

It is clear that the effective competitive negotiator seeks victory, rather than a win on the merits. The ethical component that ought to underlie the process is of little concern to the competitive negotiator. Success of this style depends on the ability to create sufficient pressure and tension to induce an emotional reaction in the opponent and to lead to a reduction in the opponent's expectation of what can be accomplished. If the pressure is inappropriate to the person or setting, the style can lead to a termination of the proceedings. In such cases, the style is ineffective. These negotiators are marked by their lack of experience, or worse yet, lack of talent.

A Lawyer's Guide to Effective Negotiation and Mediation, CLE edition, is the abridged version of the looseleaf edition designed for use in CLE programs. The section and form numbering from the looseleaf edition have been retained in the CLE edition.

Notes

The ineffective competitive negotiator tends to be intolerant, rigid and impatient. Ineffective competitive negotiators complain, are unreasonable and appear insincere because they are so. They depend on bluffs, since they are generally unprepared on the facts of the case or the law. Their hostile and rude nature is their sword.

Like their effective counterpart, the ineffective competitive negotiator is most egotistical, but to the point of being suspicious and distrustful. Their high opening demands are tainted by threats, but they are not as convincing, analytical or perceptive as their effective counterparts. In effect, ineffective competitives are unethical in their behavior and low in their trustworthiness.

They often lack social skills and graces which, when compounded with their lack of analytical skills, appear to be argumentative and are irritating to others. *Id.* at 99. Not appearing sociable or likeable challenges the credibility of the negotiator. Once a negotiator loses credibility in the process, there is little hope for success. Essentially, once a negotiator is not perceived to be credible by the others with whom an agreement must be reached, his positions and requests are seen with skepticism. Perhaps because it raises fundamental questions about the character of the negotiator, the ineffective competitive negotiator risks losing the interpersonal relationships both in the negotiation and thereafter.

Competitiveness is an innate quality which drives the person, whether effectively or not, vis-a-vis the other negotiator and the nature of the matter and issues. The competitive negotiator is driven to win and winning means conceding as little as possible but obtaining as much as possible. The assessment of a case made by the competitive negotiator will likely be higher in terms of establishing base needs and goal boundaries, not that the terms will be unfair or unrealistic. Rather, the terms sought will be higher in comparison to those a less competitive negotiator would draw.

The competitive negotiator can be strikingly successful when exploring settlement terms with a person who is

A Lawyer's Guide to Effective Negotiation and Mediation, CLE edition, is the abridged version of the looseleaf edition designed for use in CLE programs. The section and form numbering from the looseleaf edition have been retained in the CLE edition.

48

less prepared on the case, less informed about negotiation style, and not adept at adjusting to the strategic efforts of the competitive negotiator. On the other hand, the competitive negotiator who comes up against a skilled, astute and prepared opponent will be driven either to deadlock or into a reconsideration of position. In the latter case, the competitive negotiator becomes frustrated with the other negotiator and may erect barriers in the process.

Negotiators marked by their competitive style can generate an increased tension level and sense of mistrust in the negotiation. These variables can jeopardize the interpersonal relationships between the negotiators and the parties whom they represent. *Id.* at 100. The consequence of the intimidation in negotiation can be damage to the immediate case as it moves towards trial. For example, anger triggered in the negotiators or parties can lead the players further away from a possible settlement.

The sense of distrust can lead the negotiators to overstate the extent of agreement and disagreement which can lead the competitive negotiators to lead others to believe that they are closer to agreement than they really are. Moreover, when a competitive negotiator improperly senses agreement in their opponents, they will begin to increase their demands and expectations in the negotiation, although such may not be appropriate or justifiable. The result is the negotiation may break down.

The competitive negotiator can be identified by phrases such as: "Why do you need that?" or "Are you crazy, you don't really think my client will ever give that up do you?" The vocal tone accompanying these phrases suggests challenge and can lead to arguments. Of course, the cooperative negotiator may feel badly that the opponent is upset; the reality is that the comments are little more than a tactic to gain or maintain control in the negotiation. The recipient of these types of comments needs to be sensitive to shifting the conversation back to issues and rational thinking.

While it is not easy to bring an innately competitive negotiator into the cooperative style of negotiation, the

A Lawyer's Guide to Effective Negotiation and Mediation, CLE edition, is the abridged version of the looseleaf edition designed for use in CLE programs. The section and form numbering from the looseleaf edition have been retained in the CLE edition.

cooperative negotiator may best be able to accomplish this through recognizing the interests and goals formally in the interaction. Such a maneuver is carefully handled by the cooperative negotiator.

§ 4.3   The Cooperative Negotiator

Many people assume that ethics and propriety require only cooperative tactics in negotiation, and they believe cooperation to be the only effective road towards resolution. Cooperatives feel a high commitment to reasonable and fair negotiation; they do not view the process as a game. Cooperative negotiators assume negotiation presents an opportunity in which both sides can succeed or win. They seek to negotiate in an objective, fair, and trustworthy manner. To maneuver against the opponent's emotions is to be inappropriately manipulative and this goes against the natural grain of the cooperative negotiator.

Cooperative negotiators rely on communication as they seek to uncover the interests, values and attitudes which all parties share and want an open exchange of information to further a mutual search for resolution. In reality, the nature of negotiation between advocates in an adversarial setting brings into conflict dual motivations: the competitive drive to be an advocate and to maximize one's clients rewards, and the countering cooperative desire to reach a solution which is fair to all parties.

While the competitive negotiator focuses on the first motivation, the cooperative can reconcile both objectives. Cooperation should not be viewed as the better approach; rather it is simply a different route to resolution from the competitive mindset. Like the competitive negotiator, there are effective and ineffective cooperative negotiators.

Effective cooperative negotiators appear to have certain identifiable objectives when they negotiate: (1) they have a need to be ethical and professionally responsible; (2) they want a maximum settlement for their client but only if this can be accomplished in a fair and ethical manner; (3) they wish to meet their client's needs outside the courtroom if possible and with the preservation of the

A Lawyer's Guide to Effective Negotiation and Mediation, CLE edition, is the abridged version of the looseleaf edition designed for use in CLE programs. The section and form numbering from the looseleaf edition have been retained in the CLE edition.

interpersonal relationships with their opponents. Larry L. Teply, *Legal Negotiation in a Nutshell* (West Publishing, 1991) at 91; Gerald Williams, *Legal Negotiation and Settlement* (West Publishing, 1983).

The effective cooperative negotiator is perceived to be fair. She is sociable, tactful and friendly. She will move off of a position to consider other realistic options. Their goal is to facilitate agreement in the absence of threat and with a sensitivity to the needs of their clients. They are willing to share information with their opponents.

An ineffective cooperative negotiator is also seen to be fair and trustworthy, but may volunteer too much information by giving power to her opponent. Because they lack the skills and attitudes of being perceptive, creative or organized, ineffective cooperative negotiators can be perceived as being unsure of their position and of the value of the case. Thus, while the effective cooperative is no pushover in negotiation, the ineffective cooperative negotiator can be swayed in a direction not in the best interests of their clients.

The cooperative negotiator moves psychologically *toward* the opposing attorney in an effort to uncover common ground or mutuality of interest. The cooperative style is evidenced in a sense of shared interests, values and attitudes between all parties. The cooperative negotiator uses rational and logical positions designed and offered to obtain the cooperation of the others. Cooperative negotiators operate in an atmosphere they perceive to be trusting and in which no one is assumed to seek a special advantage for their own position or that of their clients.

The underlying intent of the cooperative negotiator is to achieve fairness in the terms of resolution; these terms should be reached from an objective analysis of all the facts and relevant law. The cooperative negotiator needs to avoid being vulnerable to exploitation. A cooperative negotiator who appears weak to a competitive opponent risks losing their image and ability to maintain a position. After all, the competitive negotiator will seek concessions from the cooperative; if the cooperative gives

A Lawyer's Guide to Effective Negotiation and Mediation, CLE edition, is the abridged version of the looseleaf edition designed for use in CLE programs. The section and form numbering from the looseleaf edition have been retained in the CLE edition.

up several things, he may be left with little to trade prior to the negotiation reaching the final stages of compromise.

As is true with the competitive negotiator, the description of a negotiator as being cooperative in style reflects the psychological view of that person. The cooperative negotiator understands that she is cooperative and feels more comfortable using cooperative techniques of fact gathering and creation of solution over threat and argument. Unlike the competitive negotiator who may knowingly exercise cooperative skills and tactics in order to gain trust and control, the cooperative negotiator is, more often than not, uncomfortable exercising competitive tactics. Competitive tactics are likely to create anxiety for the cooperative negotiator because they trigger challenge, not mutual cooperation. The cooperative negotiator can be very effective so long as he is sensitive to the fact that not every negotiator shares the desire to find a win-win resolution. In some ways, the success of a cooperative negotiator relies on the joint effort of the other negotiators. If all negotiators are cooperative in style, then the likely outcome is a set of terms with which all parties can live. Candidly, the negotiator who simply appears to be cooperative but never works jointly towards uncovering areas of mutual interest, can produce final terms that are one-sided.

Thus, honesty and truth of disclosure, while components of an ethical interaction, cannot be assumed or presumed; to do so would be naive within the boundaries of an adversarial system. Certainly, cooperation in intent is a noble goal, but style is reflective of innate character; not everyone possesses the quality of cooperation. The absence of cooperativeness in a person is not a flaw in character, just a reflection of a differing set of values and motivation mechanisms.

The cooperative negotiator is likely to ask a question such as: "Will these terms meet your client's needs?" or to state: "Help me understand how I can create a proposal that provides what you want to have out of this session. . ." These comments indicate the fair and rea-

A Lawyer's Guide to Effective Negotiation and Mediation, CLE edition, is the abridged version of the looseleaf edition designed for use in CLE programs. The section and form numbering from the looseleaf edition have been retained in the CLE edition.

sonable approach which is the mark of the cooperative negotiator. The competitive negotiator will hear these statements as an opportunity to gain control; the cooperative will be appreciative of the offer for mutual effort to reach resolution.

The exercise of the two extremes of negotiation style does sometimes raise the question: is either style "better" or "more right" than the other? Thus, while most negotiators fall somewhere between the extremes, the distinction between the styles creates the ever-present question about the more desireable of the styles.

§ 4.5 Identifying Negotiation Style

Evaluating negotiator style necessitates a study of those components which reflect it: personality, values, demeanor, conduct, and the circumstances which surround the negotiation interaction. It is not advisable to exercise tactics which are unnatural to the negotiator's style; a person cannot be what he is not designed to be. Negotiators can evaluate their own style, and that of others, along two dimensions: (1) natural personality, and (2) the ability to employ particular tactics in particular negotiation sessions and with individual negotiators. Each facet of the analysis requires careful consideration.

Part of the importance in understanding the style of all negotiators is that success will be a reflection of such understanding. Client satisfaction and future business in an increasingly complex legal market means more sophisticated tools throughout the litigation process. In negotiation, being able to identify and meet the components of style is but one basic element of success in the process.

First, a negotiator can evaluate the degree to which his personality and demeanor enable an effective exercise of competitive or cooperative tactics. This evaluation is underlined by the competitive negotiator's little felt need to uncover the needs or interests of the other, and the cooperative person's need to feel right in the negotiation by, at a minimum, seeking to meet the needs of the other. This basic determination, once identified, is fundamental

A Lawyer's Guide to Effective Negotiation and Mediation, CLE edition, is the abridged version of the looseleaf edition designed for use in CLE programs. The section and form numbering from the looseleaf edition have been retained in the CLE edition.

Notes

to the selection of tactics the negotiator may choose to exercise.

A negotiator's selected tactics will either reflect her underlying competitive or cooperative natural style or demonstrate a style which is different from her own to some degree. It is not difficult to see why the competitive negotiator may use cooperative tactics to invite the other negotiator's candor and openness. The actual underlying motive, however, is to gain as much information as possible from the unsuspecting and assumably cooperative opponent.

The more difficult identification is the cooperative negotiator who may choose to employ a competitive tactic, such as threat or anger. One possible scenario is a cooperative negotiator's perceived need to exhibit strength in response to persistent challenges in the negotiation. In addition, the cooperative negotiator may seek a balance against a strong opposing competitive style. It is certainly less likely that a cooperative negotiator will see the need to use competitive tactics than it is for a competitive negotiator to seize an opportunity for control through apparent cooperation.

Evaluation of negotiator style also needs to include a consideration of the circumstances which surround the negotiation. These circumstances include the history of relations between the parties, the lawyers, and the parties and lawyers. Obviously, underlying motives of revenge or otherwise poor relations can trigger barriers to the interaction and highlight the style employed. The timing of the case can also affect the way in which style is exhibited.

A case close to trial can trigger impatience or desperation; a court date well in the future may lead to laid back conduct that either is or is not open to a cooperative effort toward resolution. Pressure placed on the negotiators, whether from an internal or external source, can impact on the techniques employed.

Because tactics may or may not accurately reflect negotiation style, it is important to incorporate environ-

A Lawyer's Guide to Effective Negotiation and Mediation, CLE edition, is the abridged version of the looseleaf edition designed for use in CLE programs. The section and form numbering from the looseleaf edition have been retained in the CLE edition.

mental or situational components into the process of style identification. This component often explains perceived inconsistencies in style which seemingly appear over the course of a few negotiations. In reality, the negotiators are likely consistent in operating within the boundaries of their instinct; they are simply adjusting to relational and other factors which necessitate modification for success. Thus, the style, identification and evaluation processes are complex endeavors which need to be evaluated beyond negotiator reputation or single-faceted conduct.

Effectiveness of technique varies with the character, disposition and skills of the negotiator; an analysis of negotiator personality and skill provides a more useful focus for negotiation preparation than does dwelling on whether one's style falls neatly into one category or the other.

Knowing one's own style is clearly important for determining which tactics and techniques will be the most effective. Just as important is to seek an understanding of the styles of the other negotiators against whom (for the competitive) or with whom (for the cooperative) the negotiation will occur. Absent this knowledge, a negotiator becomes vulnerable to the control tactics of others and the unmoving demands of competitive negotiators.

Many people react in a positive manner to others who approach them with an air of openness and cooperation. Moreover, negotiators will often naturally adopt and mirror back the approach of the opponent, perhaps to establish balance and insure a more workable setting. Human nature dictates that one who acts competitively will likely meet similarity in response from the other. However, such reaction is not true in all cases. The reason lies within a distinction between negotiator style and the tactics employed.

Intent and appearance are very different things. Consider whether the reaction to a negotiator's style is a reflection of personality, or simply a tactic in itself. For example, one seemingly cooperative tactic employed by a lawyer was to send a copy of a well-known book on negotiation to his opponents. The book promotes mutual coop-

---

A Lawyer's Guide to Effective Negotiation and Mediation, CLE edition, is the abridged version of the looseleaf edition designed for use in CLE programs. The section and form numbering from the looseleaf edition have been retained in the CLE edition.

eration between negotiators towards a win-win result. He would routinely send a copy of that text to the opponents with whom he had never before negotiated. Charles B. Craver, *Effective Legal Negotiation and Settlement* (Michie Company, 1986) at 47. This naturally competitive lawyer used a seemingly cooperative tactic to convey an image of cooperation to the opponent. In reality, his desire was to create a negotiation interaction which would permit him to "clean out" the naively trusting opponent.

The likelihood of misidentifying a negotiator's style is high. It is likely the case that an evaluation of any negotiator's style will need to be made over the course of several negotiations. Lawyers in the same firm might share their evaluations of a specific opponent in order to deepen their understanding of that lawyer's negotiation style. The viability of this evaluation assumes that the associated lawyers have an accurate understanding of their own negotiation style. Obviously, an inaccurate data base will consequently reduce the validity of the evaluation of the targeted lawyer/negotiator.

Since lawyers often find themselves negotiating with the same opponents over and over again, the long term benefits of style evaluation are clearly worth the effort over time necessarily expended to achieve a viable analysis. Impressions on style will change from negotiation to negotiation and in the course of each negotiation. Over time, however, patterns of consistency will emerge and ability to predict tactics and counter them will improve.

The long term result should be increasingly successful results in negotiations with opponents due to a sophisticated knowledge of that opponent's style and technique. The incorporation of this knowledge into negotiation preparation is essential and fundamental.

The effective negotiator monitors the style and tactics of the opponent from the beginning to the end of each negotiation session. Successful analysis means distinguishing reality from appearance. The necessary and perhaps unfortunate need is for each negotiator to maintain skepticism about the real motivation and intent of the other

A Lawyer's Guide to Effective Negotiation and Mediation, CLE edition, is the abridged version of the looseleaf edition designed for use in CLE programs. The section and form numbering from the looseleaf edition have been retained in the CLE edition.

negotiator. In the best of worlds, all negotiators will cooperate towards a fair, equitable and mutually satisfying agreement; unfortunately, we do not live in the best of worlds. What appears from one negotiation to be cooperation, may in reality be a competitive maneuver. The aware negotiator never loses track of the need to monitoring for reality.

A negotiator may choose to change course during a negotiation. If cooperative tactics do not advance the discussion, a touch of competitive anger may trigger a positive shift. As each negotiator evaluates and adjusts to the style of the other, the interpersonal dynamics will lead each negotiator, in most cases, to try different tactics until she senses an appropriate degree of presence and control.

It is likely clear at this point that negotiation style and tactics are not evaluated in a vacuum. They are flexible and adjustable to the particular opponents and the stage of the negotiation. Tactics which may be effective and appropriate later in the process may be detrimental to final results if employed earlier on, and vice-versa.

Determining which tactics to exercise at what point of the negotiation requires an understanding of the progressive stages of the process. Once the stages of negotiation are set out, it is an easier task to consider how different negotiators select tactics from among the arsenal of available tactics to be the most effective negotiator possible.

*

A Lawyer's Guide to Effective Negotiation and Mediation, CLE edition, is the abridged version of the looseleaf edition designed for use in CLE programs. The section and form numbering from the looseleaf edition have been retained in the CLE edition.

Chapter 5

STAGES OF NEGOTIATION

Table of Sections

WESTLAW Electronic Research

See WESTLAW Electronic Research Guide preceding the Summary of Contents.

Notes

§ 5.1   Overview of the Process

Every negotiation progresses through a series of phases from the orientation of and between the negotiators through a conclusion of the session, whether by agreement or breakdown. An understanding of this progression enables the negotiators to monitor both the interaction and the conduct of the other negotiators, relative to the phase of the negotiation.

While every negotiation progresses through the same stages, they do not each move smoothly from one stage to the next. Rather, they may backstep to meet a need that arises. Each step of the process is impacted by certain factors which include:

(1) **Prior Negotiation History Between the Negotiators.** People who have negotiated with each other in the past have expectations of the values, attitudes and behaviors of their opponent; they have an instinct based in experience of how others will respond to their own

---

A Lawyer's Guide to Effective Negotiation and Mediation, CLE edition, is the abridged version of the looseleaf edition designed for use in CLE programs. The section and form numbering from the looseleaf edition have been retained in the CLE edition.

Notes

style, strategy and tactics. This knowledge can shorten orientation and initial positioning maneuvers.

→ (2) **Other History Between the Negotiators.** Although the negotiators may not have negotiated with each other in the past, they may share other history, such as experience as classmates, friends or relatives. In this case, a negotiator may have significant knowledge about the other person's natural reactions and expectations of conduct. These people have more at risk than the negotiation itself; their ongoing relationship is potentially on the line.

Many phases can be shortened as a result of personal history, but a prior relationship between the negotiators can also give rise to ethical concerns, such as an appearance of impropriety to clients. The possibility of any conflict must be disclosed to clients; close relations between lawyers may, in and of themselves, preclude negotiation of terms until one lawyer withdraws. In no case should expediency of the process be permitted to replace propriety of lawyer conduct.

→ (3) **Nature of the Case.** The specific facts of a case or a negotiator's experience level with a type of case can shape the nature and length of the negotiation. For example, where an opponent lacks experience in an area of the law, he may bow to the experience of the other. They may reach an agreement prematurely, circumventing some or all stages of the negotiation but possibly to the detriment of the client.

Conversely, where both negotiators share an expertise in the area of law involved in the negotiation, much time may be spent arguing philosophy of law and attempting one-upmanship. The result of such arguments may be a delay in the process that cannot progress until the negotiators return the focus of their discussion to the practical components of the discussion, i.e., the issues and terms of settlement.

→ (4) **Location of the Negotiation.** The atmosphere or conditions in which the negotiation is conducted can structure the manner of the negotiation. A setting perceived by one or more negotiators to be uncomfortable

A Lawyer's Guide to Effective Negotiation and Mediation, CLE edition, is the abridged version of the looseleaf edition designed for use in CLE programs. The section and form numbering from the looseleaf edition have been retained in the CLE edition.

60

will create an advantage in the negotiation for the person who established the setting. Hard chairs, no coffee or broken air conditioning can lead negotiators to become aggravated or angry in tone or word, thus shortening the process and lessening the likelihood for agreement.

(5) **Physical or Mental Condition of the Negotiators.** Everyone has their better and worse days. A negotiation scheduled after a negotiator has had an argument at home or at the office, or when a negotiator is ill or tired, creates unbalance in the interaction. The discomfort can be capitalized by a sharp and well conditioned opponent.

The negotiator experiencing physical or psychological difficulty is best advised to postpone the session until the interfering condition is resolved. The reason for the postponement need not be disclosed, but if requested, the negotiator may wish to state that personal conflicts necessitate a short postponement.

§ 5.2 Stage One—Orientation, Positioning and Attitudinal Bargaining

The negotiation begins with each negotiator feeling out the other, in terms of persona or image. For example, a negotiator who boasts of her experience with the type of litigation involved in the case, or the years of practice she brings to the negotiation, or even the level of responsibility she has at her office, establishes a character to be played out in the negotiation. The dynamics of the orientation set the pace and tone for the entire session. Negotiators may shift their technique as the process proceeds, but any such shift will be in response to the interaction between the initial identities and styles established by each negotiator.

The negotiating relationship that emerges during the orientation phase will reflect whether the negotiators are enacting competitive or cooperative styles, or some mix of the two. See Chapter Four. Each negotiator tries to anticipate the strategies and tactics likely to be used by the other negotiators; the interaction and reactions of the negotiators can lead to changes in behavior that may or may

A Lawyer's Guide to Effective Negotiation and Mediation, CLE edition, is the abridged version of the looseleaf edition designed for use in CLE programs. The section and form numbering from the looseleaf edition have been retained in the CLE edition.

61

not prove to be reflective of each negotiator's predominant style.

Orientation is a period for testing positions. Negotiators meeting for the first time compare business cards, war stories, and who they each know of prominence. They probe each other's law school backgrounds, grades, and scholarly accomplishments. This is interesting since a study by Craver revealed no correlation between negotiating skills and law school performance. Charles B. Craver, *Legal Negotiation and Settlement* (Michie Company, 1986), xii.

Yet, lawyers seem never to discount the lasting impact of law school memories. Nevertheless, the scope and nature of preliminary discussion reflects the testing and maneuvering of atmosphere and image between the negotiators.

The style of the negotiators should be evidenced in their conduct, absent an intentional effort to use tactics which are opposite to the style reflected. The cooperative negotiator, for example, is initially uncomfortable negotiating with someone she does not know. A cooperative negotiator's conduct is likely to include accommodation, sociability and politeness because she wishes to be seen as trustworthy. This person will use the first portion of a negotiation session to establish trust, cooperation and mutual respect. In fact, the cooperative negotiator experiences difficulty when others act aggressively, since this behavior type is uncomfortable for her to mimic or match.

The competitive negotiator, to the contrary, will use initial conversation to uncover the nature and extent of the opponent's resources. Bad jokes, humorous anecdotes or poor puns are not unusual attempts to ease existing tension, or change the direction of the conversation. Gerard I. Nierenberg, *Fundamentals of Negotiating* (Harper & Row, 1973) at 55.

Initial negotiation dialogue is often strained, reflecting the difference in posture of the two sides. For example, the competitive negotiator approaches the other competitively, but the cooperative negotiator mirrors the

A Lawyer's Guide to Effective Negotiation and Mediation, CLE edition, is the abridged version of the looseleaf edition designed for use in CLE programs. The section and form numbering from the looseleaf edition have been retained in the CLE edition.

approach of the other. Charles B. Craver, *Legal Negotiation and Settlement* (Michie Company, 1986) at 50. If the orientation between the negotiators shifts to a significantly competitive dialogue, effort is needed to ignite a discussion to uncover mutual interests.

At this early stage of the negotiation, the negotiators may not have access to all facts; answers to legal questions may still be outstanding, or in dispute. Even with existing uncertainty, the negotiators proceed to set out some position. It is important to permit leeway in whatever position is stated during the initial moments of the negotiation so each negotiator can meet the psychological need of give and take. Gerald R. Williams, *Legal Negotiation and Settlement* (West Publishing, 1983) at 73.

If the conversation during orientation becomes markedly competitive or strained, it may be necessary for one side to engage in "attitudinal bargaining" with the other. Charles B. Craver, *Legal Negotiation and Settlement* (Michie Company, 1986) at 50. Put differently, attitudinal bargaining is useful when one negotiator appears overtly competitive or rigid.

Attitudinal bargaining is the process of confronting an abrasive or otherwise competitive opponent with questions that bring the conduct into the open. Questions such as "Why are you being so uncooperative?" or more bluntly, "What kind of an attitude is that?" exemplify the concept. They call immediate attention to the perceived difficulty in approach. Not taking an affirmative step to challenge the exhibited conduct will mean continued overt competition. Realistically, the perceived intent of the questioner who challenges behavior which accompanies attitudinal bargaining is more important than the response to the questions posed.

In fact, the response to the rhetorical questions may not provide immediate relief, but at a minimum, establish for the user of the technique, a foothold in shifting the direction of the negotiation. In short, attitudinal bargaining encourages and guides the other side to be more cooperative. *Id.,* at 49.

A Lawyer's Guide to Effective Negotiation and Mediation, CLE edition, is the abridged version of the looseleaf edition designed for use in CLE programs. The section and form numbering from the looseleaf edition have been retained in the CLE edition.

Notes

Conduct deemed to be detrimental to progressive negotiations may or may not be reflective of that negotiator's actual style. Inexperienced negotiators may believe they should act in a certain way, others may be exploring new dimensions of their own style, and still others may simply misread the situation. In the worst case scenario, the negotiator may be socially inept. The point is that people should be given the opportunity to shift their approach without repercussion, when that shift provides or returns a positive tone to the discussion.

In some cases, then, attitudinal bargaining may be more of an interaction adjustment mechanism. The one who uses the technique needs to monitor the response. If there is an immediate response, then the modified behavior may be a more accurate reflection of the user's natural style. If the original behavior does not change, then a decision needs to be made as to whether the negotiation can proceed or whether a postponement would better serve the parties' needs, until the lawyers can agree to work in a reasonable manner.

Once initial relations are established between the negotiators, they may then use one of three strategies available to set out an opening position.

(1) **Maximum Positioning.** The negotiator asks for more than she actually expects to get. This essentially competitive approach hides the bargainer's minimum expectations and reasonable limits. It also prevents a commitment to an overly modest appraisal. The value of this strategy lies in its underlying potential for the opponent to later reduce his expectations.

For example, if the opponent has not properly appraised the case, a stated high demand may serve as a benchmark for the discussion. Gerald R. Williams, *Legal Negotiation and Settlement* (West Publishing, 1983) at 74–75. Conversely, the maximalist who refuses to shift off of an initial position may become unreasonably fixed on that position. The greater the level of commitment a negotiator has to a position, the more she will need to de-

---

fend that position in the negotiation. In addition, the more the lawyer's ego becomes integrated into the process.

⟶ (2) **Equitable Positioning.** This strategy is predominantly cooperative in approach. The proponent illustrates a commitment to reaching a resolution and creating the expectation that all negotiators will work together towards reaching an amicable resolution. Concessions tend to be made early on in the negotiation under this approach because a greater reliance by the user is placed on trust. Gerald R. Williams, *Legal Negotiation and Settlement* (West Publishing, 1983) at 75–76.

If the opposition is inexperienced or lacks the authority to settle without approval of a superior, that person will not settle until he perceives a sense of victory. As such, opponents will be hard pressed to accept any initial proposal presented, regardless of the degree of reasonableness. Gerard I. Nierenberg, *Fundamentals of Negotiating* (Harper & Row, 1973) at 56.

(3) **Integrative Positioning.** This strategy consists of focusing initially on the interests which underlie each negotiator's position, rather than addressing the positions themselves. Gerald R. Williams, *Legal Negotiation and Settlement* (West Publishing, 1983) at 76–77; Roger Fisher & W. Ury, *Getting to Yes* (Penguin Press, 1983) at 11.

The term "integrative positioning" is something of a misnomer because the approach actually avoids the establishment of an initial position altogether. Each negotiator's initial statements or "positions" are not considered to be inflexible. *Id.,* at 55. The approach anticipates that concessions will be made by all negotiators. This approach is most likely used in a case which involves multiple issues or issues of a complex nature. Gerald R. Williams, *Legal Negotiation and Settlement* (West Publishing, 1983) at 77.

§ 5.3 Stage Two—Information Exchange and Control: Competition

The goal of every negotiator is to uncover the other negotiator's bottom line, i.e., the terms of settlement that

A Lawyer's Guide to Effective Negotiation and Mediation, CLE edition, is the abridged version of the looseleaf edition designed for use in CLE programs. The section and form numbering from the looseleaf edition have been retained in the CLE edition.

will be least costly, but nevertheless be acceptable to the other party. As a result, the initial exchange of information is, by definition, a competitive activity. Each negotiator should be focused on obtaining information about the other side's position and interest; simultaneously, the negotiator needs to control the disclosure of details of his own position.

The concept is important: the more information one gathers about the other side's position, the more control there is over the interaction. The manner in which the negotiator's bottom line is sought will vary with negotiator questioning style. The competitive negotiator, for example, will work hard, directly and with consistency to find the opponent's bottom line.

The cooperative negotiator, however, may encourage and facilitate a thorough exchange of ideas and interests so that the negotiators may achieve an agreement which can be viewed by all to be fair. Donald G. Gifford, *Legal Negotiation Theory and Applications* (West Publishing, 1989) at 120–21. The cooperative negotiator often risks conceding more information than is necessary; this reflects the cooperative's desire for fairness and is a reflection of human nature to be helpful. The nearly certain result from extensive information disclosure by a negotiator is the creation of a disadvantage to that negotiator's bargaining leverage and transfer of power through information to the recipients of information.

Maintaining awareness of and control over the disclosures one makes in a negotiation may be the single most important factor in the process. Without intent to downplay the importance of guarding concessions or handling nonverbal tactics and strategies, the amount and nature of information disclosed becomes the basis for the terms discussed and negotiated. Once information is put on the table, it cannot be taken back. Unlike the jury which can be instructed by a judge *not* to consider certain testimony, the effective negotiator listens, evaluates and integrates each piece of information into a whole.

A Lawyer's Guide to Effective Negotiation and Mediation, CLE edition, is the abridged version of the looseleaf edition
designed for use in CLE programs. The section and form numbering from the looseleaf edition
have been retained in the CLE edition.

The consistency, coherence and completeness of the integration of information is evaluated by the effective negotiator, as a jury would evaluate each party's story. Negotiators should keep the storytelling model in mind not only as a tool of preparation, but as a guidepost for disclosure. Information that triggers inconsistency or a gap in the negotiator's position can lead to problems for that negotiator.

Positions and terms are established and challenged from the negotiator's information disclosures; thus, each bit of information released by a negotiator should be made knowingly and with an awareness of its potential effect on the direction of the negotiation. The negotiator who approaches the exchange of information in each negotiation as a competitive exercise can gain a decided advantage in the process.

The more information one gathers from the opponent, the greater potential for control is gained for the remainder of the negotiation. Ultimately, the final terms of the agreement will be a reflection of the information exchanged through the process.

The protection over the disclosure of information does not mean that negotiators should attempt to conceal everything. Obviously, everyone needs to partake in the interaction or there will be no negotiation. Moreover, there are practical limits on how much information one negotiator can get an opponent to disclose without offering disclosure in return.

Each negotiator needs to disclose information sufficient to facilitate the process; the underlying intent should be to encourage the other negotiators to make disclosures of both fact and need. Each disclosure permits the negotiators to evaluate and integrate the information with every other piece of disclosed information as the story of the party becomes clear.

The negotiators should listen carefully to what everyone else says, interjecting comments to reflect understanding of the other side's position. The importance and value of other negotiator's disclosures should be em-

A Lawyer's Guide to Effective Negotiation and Mediation, CLE edition, is the abridged version of the looseleaf edition designed for use in CLE programs. The section and form numbering from the looseleaf edition have been retained in the CLE edition.

67

phasized; the positive reaction will encourage further disclosure from that person. Comments such as: "I understand now what you are looking for; can you clarify why you seek that term?" or "That's interesting, but I still don't see the importance of that issue yet, perhaps you can clarify it," are supportive and inviting of additional information. Contrary to eliciting disclosure from others, care needs to be exerted to protect against making damaging disclosures.

There are techniques available to negotiators who wish to limit the disclosures they make during the early stages of a negotiation. These techniques can be used in response to information-seeking questions asked by an opponent. They include:

(1) Change the subject. If a fact is requested by one negotiator that is considered by the other to be best left undisclosed at the time, then the negotiator can choose not to answer it. Instead, the negotiator can use some element of the question or request to shift the focus of the inquiry back to the other side. For example, if asked: "Can you accept a figure less than $10,000?" the negotiator might respond: "Is that the limit of your authority today?" This response shifts the inquiry over to the other side and actually serves to obtain rather than disclose information.

(2) Answer a different, but related question. For example, if asked: "Would your client consider a replacement product?" One could respond: "I do know my client needs to be properly compensated." This leaves the responsibility on the questioner to either follow up the original inquiry, or to accept as meaningful the seemingly responsive answer.

(3) Answer incompletely, disclosing as little as possible, but nevertheless responding to the question. Brief or limited answers ("Yes" or "No") often suffice. This requires the questioner to follow up with more open-ended or probing questions to expand the extent of disclosure.

(4) Delay the response by promising that an answer will be provided at a later time, once necessary but miss-

---

A Lawyer's Guide to Effective Negotiation and Mediation, CLE edition, is the abridged version of the looseleaf edition designed for use in CLE programs. The section and form numbering from the looseleaf edition have been retained in the CLE edition.

68

ing information is gathered. This gives the questioner the chance to pursue the question from a different angle, or to assist in the gathering of the needed information. The questioner does need to analyze whether the delay is legitimate or simply a desire to gain time for some other purpose.

(5) Offer to answer the question, but only after the other negotiator answers an inquiry stated as being a prerequisite to the initial inquiry. This response seeks to maintain a balance of control and power in the negotiation.

(6) Avoid including in the response any information which the other side would likely have an interest in knowing. Disclosures can be limited to only that information which is necessary to provide a response. Moreover, each response should include a request to the other negotiator for information along with specifying why that information is necessary. Donald G. Gifford, *Legal Negotiation Theory and Applications* (West Publishing, 1989) at 136–38. Then, the latter request for new information need be adhered to until any further disclosures are made.

It may be frustrating for the cooperative negotiator to have difficulty in obtaining helpful disclosures during the early moments of the negotiation. Unfortunately, there are few negotiations in which the preliminary jockeying of position can be avoided. Eventually, the negotiators will have a sense of the style of the other(s) and one person or another will offer a point from which realistic discussions can begin. This is the point at which the first meaningful proposal is offered for consideration.

§ 5.5 Stage Three—Confirming Positions With Principle

During stage three of the negotiation, the negotiators (1) discuss a real proposal, (2) should be prepared to state a position, (3) control their arsenal of possible concessions, and (4) monitor the concessions made by the other negotiator. Perhaps most important, each stated position or request for a concession should be accompanied by an underlying and supporting rationale. If one is not provided as part of the statement, then it should be requested

A Lawyer's Guide to Effective Negotiation and Mediation, CLE edition, is the abridged version of the looseleaf edition designed for use in CLE programs. The section and form numbering from the looseleaf edition have been retained in the CLE edition.

69

by the other negotiator. This exchange is important during this stage because the third stage of negotiation is marked by competition, little trust between the negotiators, and a desire for better positioning.

Since the psychology of negotiation requires a give and take, each offer or demand above or below the level anticipated will meet efforts for modification by the others. In most cases, demands will be pushed down and offers pulled up. Peace of mind requires this give and take; neither side feels it has accomplished something through the process unless each obtains a concession from the other. This dynamic operates to create equity and fairness between the negotiators.

Given the ever-present intent by negotiators to modify any stated position, it is important that each proposal be underlined with a supporting factual foundation. A position that is easily refuted because it is not granted in principle and does little more than attribute motive or intent to the other negotiator, is best not stated. The process of incorporating justification and underlying reason into a demand or offer serves to focus the discussion on content or issues; it moves the interaction away from personal confrontation.

The more consistent one's position is with regard to established and accepted principles, the less vulnerable that position is to attack. Roger Fisher & W. Ury, *Getting to Yes* (Penguin Press, 1983), at 86. Positions accompanied by precedent, standards of fairness or underlying merit, are much stronger substantively and more difficult for other negotiators to discard. The negotiator should evaluate and argue the legitimacy of each offered position against whatever objective criteria are available to the negotiators. These objective criteria may include: market value, how a court might decide the matter, precedent, professional standards, or community tradition. *Id.*, at 88–89.

Perhaps the importance of setting out a position and its rationale is best explained in its absence. The inability to support why a term is needed or desired prevents the

A Lawyer's Guide to Effective Negotiation and Mediation, CLE edition, is the abridged version of the looseleaf edition designed for use in CLE programs. The section and form numbering from the looseleaf edition have been retained in the CLE edition.

70

other side from evaluating the legitimacy of the request. Professionalism in negotiation places the burden for substantiation on the shoulders of the one making the demand, not on the recipient to explain why they can or cannot meet the demand. For example, a request for a non-compete clause needs better substantiation than "I believe it's standard in the industry."

The air of speculation raises uncertainty in the demand and opens the door for contradicting facts. If the recipient of the offer can refute the statement, the one making the demand risks losing credibility on that issue and perhaps in the negotiation as a whole.

Each negotiator should insure that her own position is carefully underlined and expressed with logic and support. In addition, each proposal from others should be evaluated to assure that it is similarly supported. Every proposal offered should be evaluated against a set of established objective criteria agreed upon by the negotiators, and applied similarly to all proposals. In short, every position offered should be defensible according to some agreed upon underlying principle or standard.

A position that cannot be supported by its maker, i.e., the support for which is: "Because that's the way it is," is on a certain road to rejection and possible interpersonal conflict. The effective negotiator can support and defend any presented position, or knows that the position will fall under challenge.

A request for a concession or offer, such as "Would you be able to pay an additional $5,000.00?" can be tested by asking, "Why is an additional $5,000.00 needed here?" An offer to which a negotiator wishes to withhold a response, such as: "We can give an additional three months on the contract, will that resolve it?" can be responded to with: "Please explain how you can afford the three months," or "Is there any additional flexibility in that time frame?" These inquiries not only seek underlying support, but also serve to control disclosure by shifting a request for information back to the other side. As always, the less information disclosed, the more power is retained.

A Lawyer's Guide to Effective Negotiation and Mediation, CLE edition, is the abridged version of the looseleaf edition designed for use in CLE programs. The section and form numbering from the looseleaf edition have been retained in the CLE edition.

Lisnek Effective Negotiation & Mediation—4
CLE Edition

Notes

The exchange of inquiries for underlying support can be a harmful exercise if it includes personal challenges or emotional attacks. Focused on content and interests, the process can lead to a meaningful and progressive exchange.

Information exchange, properly conducted, provides the negotiator with four techniques to help establish co-operation in this essentially competitive third stage:

(1) The negotiator should focus on the main points of each position presented and monitor the discussion to ensure that everyone's comments remain on point. Content-focused questions and exchange provide a positive momentum within the negotiation.

(2) Since negotiators' preparation includes knowledge of relevant facts and law, they need to be able to monitor each statement relative to the known facts and governing law for accuracy and viability.

(3) Negotiators should avoid making threats and personal attacks. These serve only to create a defensive atmosphere, sometimes leading negotiators to walk away from the table and the process.

(4) Negotiators' exercise of patience and silence often proves to be a sign of virtue during this phase. Since people can lose their tempers in the face of frustration, the successful negotiator will keep a level head, remain rational and logical. Silence can also serve as an extremely effective information-gathering technique as it often leads others to fill the gaps with disclosure.

Recognizing the consequences of not reaching resolution and confirming "for the record" that they hope to work towards a mutually acceptable agreement preserves a working atmosphere. This permits the negotiators to progress through an otherwise competitive phase to cooperation. See, e.g., Paul M. Lisnek, "Negotiating Your Salary and Benefits," *CBA Record* (June, 1989), at 32.

§ 5.6 Stage Four—Search for a Mutually Acceptable Solution—Cooperation

The focus of the cooperative stage is on reaching an agreeable solution. Discussion shifts toward resolving the

---

A Lawyer's Guide to Effective Negotiation and Mediation, CLE edition, is the abridged version of the looseleaf edition designed for use in CLE programs. The section and form numbering from the looseleaf edition have been retained in the CLE edition.

72

question: "How can we work this out in practical terms?"
Each negotiator needs to leave the negotiation believing
that all participants were committed to reaching a fair
and equitable agreement; this belief is often confirmed by
the fact that each negotiator will have made some concession toward the final agreement.

In effect, each negotiator senses a stake in the ultimate success of the negotiation outcome. The final agreement will usually be one which, while not necessarily ideal
for all negotiators, is at least satisfying to all concerned.

The shift into the cooperative stage follows the discussion of real offers presented by the negotiators. The
real offer, one which is perceived to be realistic and workable, permits the other negotiators to give serious consideration to its components. The stage may be triggered by
one negotiator stating: "Okay, this discussion isn't getting us anywhere. Let's consider these terms . . ."
Then, the discussion leads the negotiators to reflect offered terms against their own needs and interests. The
discussion will likely lead to proposed modification of the
offered terms or to the presentation of a counteroffer.
The cooperative stage means that all points of the discussion are assumed to be sincere and meant for thoughtful
consideration.

The essential component of the cooperative stage is
that all negotiators engage in a sincere search for a resolution. This does not mean that any proposal will be acceptable in its totality, nor does it guarantee that all negotiators will exercise cooperative tactics. Many negotiators continue to proceed in a competitive fashion during
this stage—working towards agreement, but always with
the intent to do the very best possible for the client in the
final agreement.

Legal negotiations are, by definition, competitive ex-
ercises. The element of competition is present even during the cooperative stage of the process. Although the negotiators make serious concessions and seek resolution to
the situation, they should always be assumed to be zeal-

A Lawyer's Guide to Effective Negotiation and Mediation, CLE edition, is the abridged version of the looseleaf edition
designed for use in CLE programs. The section and form numbering from the looseleaf edition
have been retained in the CLE edition.

ous advocates for their clients. The American adversary system would demand nothing less of legal advocates.

Consequently, no negotiator should be expected to concede more than is absolutely necessary to reach an agreement. For example, a negotiator should expect any concession she makes will be accepted by the other side, even if that concession is not within the realm of the recipient's need. The reason is that the concession can always be "refunded" for an additional term or returned in the event a comparable concession is requested. Every concession potentially creates an expectation of a returned concession; if the term was not necessary in the first place, its return could erase the expectation.

Thus, every negotiator hopes to leave the negotiation feeling that a mutually acceptable agreement has been reached. Each nevertheless seeks as much as possible for her client, shifting the balance of terms objectively in their favor. The effective negotiator proceeds ethically and within the bounds of professional responsibility towards an agreement in their client's best interests. An ineffective negotiator may cause a potentially viable agreement to fail because he persists in demanding additional concessions which are not within the client's needs.

After the negotiators have proposed their suggested terms, there will likely be areas in which the proposed terms are in accord and other components which are in conflict. Cooperative negotiators will recognize the areas of agreement as signs of the potential success of the negotiation; competitive negotiators will focus on getting as much as they can in the remaining issues. The existing differences need to be dealt with through a joint effort of the negotiators, or the process can break down.

§ 5.8 Stage Five—The Decisive Moment— Resolution or Breakdown

Most negotiations have a deadline, whether imposed artificially by the negotiators, set by an upcoming event, or set by the court. As the deadline approaches, a point of decision is triggered. The negotiators either create an acceptable set of terms or agree to end the session without coming to terms.

The moment of decision is often triggered by one negotiator who makes a final offer claiming, in effect, "take it or leave it." The demand should realistically be heard to present three choices: 1) take it, 2) leave it, or 3) offer another alternative. Gerald R. Williams, *Legal Negotiation and Settlement* (West Publishing, 1983) at 81. In many cases, breakdown occurs because the negotiators fail to recognize the third option.

A negotiator, unable to accept the offered terms, ought to think quickly for a new, yet previously unstated alternative. Incorporating the important components of the "final" offer from the other negotiator, there may still be hope for resolution. In any event, an offer or demand stated to be final should still be considered by the receiver as being subject to modification, if the session is reasonably close to agreement.

In most cases, there is actually no such thing as the "final and last offer." For example, a negotiator who states: "I can't see taking one cent below $5000," will most likely accept $4950 or even less. Note that acceptance of a term less than $5000 in this scenario does not require loss of credibility for the one who demands because the demand provides for leeway. "I can't see taking" is not the same as "I will not accept." The underlying need for providing leeway is clear enough—the possibility of additional concessions by the other side should always be provided for until such time as the process terminates.

§ 5.9 Making Concessions

Concession is the primary means by which agreements are made possible. Every concession should be viewed as an instrument of strategy. Negotiators enter the negotiation with differing interests and needs, but within the differences lie the opportunity for tradeoff and concession. What is important to one negotiator may be of great or no consequence to the other.

A Lawyer's Guide to Effective Negotiation and Mediation, CLE edition, is the abridged version of the looseleaf edition designed for use in CLE programs. The section and form numbering from the looseleaf edition have been retained in the CLE edition.

Notes

Uncovering the importance of negotiation terms through the negotiation discussion is the prerequisite to determining the value of concessions to the others. Whenever possible, negotiators attempt to concede items that have little or no value to them, but which meet an important need of the other. Estimating the value of a particular item to another negotiator permits a simultaneous calculation of value of item(s) which can be sought in trade. Mark K. Schoenfield and R.M. Schoenfield, *Legal Negotiations: Getting Maximum Results* (McGraw–Hill, 1988) at 301–02.

Cooperative negotiators understand and believe in the importance of making concessions; they exert great effort to create an atmosphere in which a just and equitable outcome can be achieved. By contrast, competitive negotiators seek to obtain the maximum number of concessions from their opponents while making the fewest and smallest concessions possible in return. In fact, the competitive negotiator considers any concession made to be a sign of weakness, whether in himself or in the opposition. The competitive negotiator is resistant even to the thought of giving up anything at all. Gerald R. Williams, *Legal Negotiation and Settlement* (West Publishing, 1983) at 80.

The psychological need to achieve concessions from each negotiator is therefore quite difficult in the case of the competitive negotiator. Although competitive negotiators will strive to insure that any concession they make will not be very important or substantive, their goal remains the achievement of the maximum possible outcome; yet, their grant of a concession is essential to the process. Hopefully, each negotiator can concede something she doesn't believe essential to her position, but will be perceived to be of significance by the recipient of the concession.

§ 5.10   Reaching Agreement

If the negotiators move through the moment of decision to reach an agreement, then the terms will need to be set out with clarity and specificity to insure their en-

---

A Lawyer's Guide to Effective Negotiation and Mediation, CLE edition, is the abridged version of the looseleaf edition designed for use in CLE programs. The section and form numbering from the looseleaf edition have been retained in the CLE edition.

forceability. The drafting of the final agreement is not the time to decide that one's work is over, leaving the task of drafting to the other side. All negotiators who do not participate in drafting documents embodying the resultant agreement of necessity rely on the mercy, good faith, and drafting skill of the draftsperson.

The creation of the final and binding document is a power too significant to be transferred away after a lengthy and important negotiation designed to preserve client interests. The importance of taking part in the drafting of the final agreement guards against bad faith manipulation and protects against unintended mistake.

The draftsperson can, whether by intent or mistake, use the plethora of available ambiguous legal terminology to create murkiness in the agreement. Boilerplate language, for example, can lead to the inclusion of non-negotiated items, since the final written agreement will provide the only enforceable provisions between the parties; clarity of language and specificity and accuracy of terms need to be carefully guarded by all negotiators. Harry Edwards and J. White, *The Lawyer as a Negotiator* (West Publishing, 1977) at 121.

§ 5.14 Post–Negotiation Evaluation

Growth as an effective negotiator can be furthered through an evaluation of each negotiation session. A post-negotiation evaluation should always be conducted upon completion of the process, whether or not an agreement is reached. Oftentimes, unsuccessful negotiations (those which terminate without an agreement) teach a negotiator more about her style and approach than do many "successful" efforts.

Obviously, success as a negotiator means much more than reaching an occasional agreement. It means that the best possible terms are perceived to have been obtained for the client under the circumstances. Roger S. Haydock, *Negotiation Practice* (John Wiley & Sons, 1984) at 176. It should also mean that the negotiators leave the negotiation process with their positive working relationship preserved. These negotiators should be able to work together in future cases with an underlying trust of each other's motives.

However, some negotiators have little concern for maintaining a positive relationship with other negotiators. An underlying competitive view leads these negotiators to be concerned with nothing more than getting everything possible from the process, regardless of the interpersonal cost. This view is short-sighted to be sure, given that many lawyers find themselves negotiating with the same lawyers in new cases. A destruction of trust between negotiators necessarily jeopardizes the effectiveness of their future negotiation efforts.

There may appear to be a conflict between preserving trust between adversarial negotiators, and zealously representing a client so as to obtain as much as possible for them; in reality, these two objectives are complementary. Creation of a poor working or professional relationship between negotiators will significantly inhibit both negotiators from obtaining much for the clients; the negotiators will spend their time balancing interpersonal conflicts.

In addition, the effective negotiator will always present underlying principles for their positions so as to respond substantively to any questions and objections from the other. Yet, while serving to preserve a good working relationship, setting out underlying principle is the essence of zealous client representation.

A negotiator who substitutes argument for principle, hostility for explanation, or defensiveness for assertiveness, is not a zealous advocate; clients find greater satisfaction in a lawyer who presents a position professionally and progressively. As such, negotiators need an ongoing sense of their negotiation capabilities and skills. The first step in creating this awareness is translating this theoretical information into a concrete and usable evaluation mechanism.

An accurate appraisal of a negotiation should consider the factors which likely affected the agreement reached and the process which produced the agreement:

A Lawyer's Guide to Effective Negotiation and Mediation, CLE edition, is the abridged version of the looseleaf edition designed for use in CLE programs. The section and form numbering from the looseleaf edition have been retained in the CLE edition.

(1) The extent to which the final agreement meets the needs and interests of the client;

(2) The extent to which each negotiator obtained her initial objectives;

(3) The extent to which the client played an active role in the process, in addition to making the ultimate settlement decision;

(4) The extent to which positions were presented by the negotiators with underlying principled positions;

(5) The extent to which the final agreement was based on principled positions, and not on a conflict between the egos of negotiators;

(6) The extent to which all available options were considered by the negotiators (i.e., Was there an attempt to create an innovative and integrative result?);

(7) The extent to which the final outcome bettered the client's current positions;

(8) The enforceability of the final agreement; and

(9) The extent to which each negotiator played a role in drafting and reviewing the agreement.

Id., at 177–78.

An evaluation of these factors indicates the extent to which the client's needs are met and the extent to which the lawyer's own performance can be improved in future negotiations.

Certainly, the terms of any agreement need to reflect the needs and interests of the client. Lawyers need to subordinate their own views to those of the client. This can be done by monitoring the negotiation in relation to the needs and objectives established by and with the client. While the sense of success is perceived by the negotiators throughout the process, the reflection against objective standards makes the process easier.

Clients are to be active in the negotiation planning and process; they should play an integral role with the lawyer. Clients provide the facts and details from which

A Lawyer's Guide to Effective Negotiation and Mediation, CLE edition, is the abridged version of the looseleaf edition designed for use in CLE programs. The section and form numbering from the looseleaf edition have been retained in the CLE edition.

Notes

their lawyer creates a principled position. An uninvolved client means the lawyer negotiates without the valuable guidance and viewpoint of the person for whom the negotiation is being conducted.

As the negotiation proceeds, the lawyers need to keep a sense of awareness that their clients' case is on the line, a factor more important than their own win-loss record. While the latter is of concern to every lawyer, any shift away from client interest jeopardizes the successful outcome of the specific case. The best way for the lawyer to insure that she meets her client's needs is to uncover and explore all alternatives with the client. Never being too quick to agree on a point, each lawyer should understand the implications of each option.

Greater perceived and objective success may lie in the creation of innovative ideas which get integrated into a beneficial whole. Such a result may lead clients to feel better about their final position, relative to their initial situation. There are other criteria commonly used by attorneys to evaluate negotiation which appear to be objective, but do not accurately assess either outcome *or* process. These include:

(1) Determining that a negotiation was successful solely because it fell within the client's prescribed limits or because the client claimed to be satisfied. This approach could preclude an agreement being reached that falls below these conditions, but which might otherwise be acceptable to the client.

(2) Concluding the negotiation was successful solely because the agreement closely reflects the opposition's limit or the client's initial objectives. This criteria assumes that the initial positions set out by the negotiators were based on rational and reasonable criteria.

In reality, both sides may have made inaccurate assessments of their own position or miscalculated the opposition's position or actual authority. The skilled negotiator listens carefully to all information presented during the negotiation to evaluate its accuracy and the extent to which it reflects revealed authority.

A Lawyer's Guide to Effective Negotiation and Mediation, CLE edition, is the abridged version of the looseleaf edition designed for use in CLE programs. The section and form numbering from the looseleaf edition have been retained in the CLE edition.

(3) Evaluating the final agreement against a model agreement. This approach is ineffective because objective criteria created by the attorney and client prior to the negotiation will most likely be modified and adjusted throughout the negotiation process.

Roger S. Haydock, *Negotiation Practice* (John Wiley & Sons, 1984) at 176–77.

These criteria do not suggest that client limits, client satisfaction, opposition limits and objectives, or preconceived model agreements are never to be considered. To the contrary, they can be of great value in monitoring the progress of the negotiation and as starting points from which the negotiation can be conducted. The caution advised is to avoid limiting an evaluation to these factors, limited in perspective. Once the process is understood, the negotiators can select from among an arsenal of tactics, those which they believe will be effective.

Form 5–5 is the post-negotiation evaluation form. Incorporating the terms and concepts set out here, the form is essential for each negotiator to complete after *each* negotiation. The insight gained on a consistent basis from each case is the best means to uncovering what techniques work and what techniques do not in particular situations. A technique that may be progressive in one situation, can set back the proceedings in another. Perhaps a result of the type of case, or perhaps as a reflection of the personality of the other negotiators, the form helps illustrate the idiosyncratic components of each negotiation; these can then be fit into a more general overall picture of one's negotiation style.

Once a negotiator understands her style and the process through which all negotiations will progress (in some form or another), she can review the arsenal of tactics which may be employed in particular negotiations. As the next chapter illustrates, the selection of a tactic must be a reflection of natural style and ability; unnatural behaviors are evidenced quickly to the sensitive or aware negotiator.

*

A Lawyer's Guide to Effective Negotiation and Mediation, CLE edition, is the abridged version of the looseleaf edition designed for use in CLE programs. The section and form numbering from the looseleaf edition have been retained in the CLE edition.

Form 5-5

Post–Negotiation Evaluation

Case Name _____

File No. _____

Attorney _____

1. Were you thoroughly prepared for the negotiation? If not, how could you have been better prepared?

2. How well were the client's needs met?

Consider the extent to which:
- the final agreement met the needs and interests
- each negotiator obtained their initial objectives
- the client played an active role in the process
- positions were presented as principled ones
- the final agreement was based on principled positions
- the final agreement was based on personality conflicts of the negotiators
- all available options were considered
- the final outcome bettered the client's current positions
- enforceability of the final agreement
- each negotiator played a role in the final drafting process

Notes:

Also consider but do not limit your consideration to:
- how the agreement met initial client limits
- how satisfied the client is with the decision
- how the agreement met initial opposition limits
- how well the agreement matches preconceived model agreements

Notes:

3. Consider the following questions with regards to information:
- did you obtain necessary information?
- how did the parties disclose information?

*

Form 5-5

- how much information was disclosed?
- were the parties able to avoid disclosing certain information without violating ethical standards?
- did party make any unintended verbal or nonverbal disclosures?

Notes:

4. What specific negotiation techniques were used and how were they managed in the interaction?

5. Did principles underlie each stated position?

6. Who made concessions? What was the effect on the interaction?

7. Did either party resort to unethical tactics, such as deliberate misrepresentations, to enhance its position? Were challanges made to these tactics?

8. What finally caused the parties to reach an agreement or to reject the opponent's final offer? Did the final settlement appear to benefit one party more than the other? If so, how was this result accomplished? How did each party feel about the final agreement?

*

Form 5–5 (continued)

Chapter 6

TACTICS IN NEGOTIATION

Table of Sections

WESTLAW Electronic Research

See WESTLAW Electronic Research Guide preceding the Summary of Contents.

Notes

§ 6.1 Selecting Natural and Appropriate Tactics

Once negotiators understand where their negotiation style fits along the competitive-cooperative continuum, they can best select the strategies and tactics appropriate to and consistent with that style. Whatever tactics are selected should be both natural and comfortable for the negotiator to execute when negotiating; people cannot effectively perform tactics which are unnatural for them, i.e., which are not within their skill ability.

Unnatural conduct appears to the other negotiators as little more than a planned performance; these moments are transparent to others. For example, feigning nervous anxiety or dissatisfaction when a negotiation is progressing in a favorable direction for that negotiator are tactics easily detected as phony by others. Unless negotiators who undertake a tactic inconsistent with the direction of the interaction or their own character are skilled performers, any such attempt can be expected to backfire on the user.

Of course, a negotiator may intentionally use a tactic not in accord with his style in and of itself. For example, the competitive negotiator may adopt cooperative means in order to encourage trust on the part of the other negotiator. The intent would be to create rapport, so that this

---

A Lawyer's Guide to Effective Negotiation and Mediation, CLE edition, is the abridged version of the looseleaf edition designed for use in CLE programs. The section and form numbering from the looseleaf edition have been retained in the CLE edition.

87

competitive negotiator might obtain greater concessions from an unsuspecting cooperative opponent. In this instance, cooperative tactics create an appearance that inaccurately reflects the actual style of the negotiator. Sensitivity to reaching beneath a set of used tactics is essential to uncovering the actual operative style of the negotiator.

Conversely, an opponent who consciously recognizes or subconsciously perceives that another negotiator is performing, may lose any sense of trust that had previously been established. In effect the opponent sees through the tactic (likely cooperative) to see the actual style (competitive). This scenario is most likely because an opponent will always have a guard up to competitive tactics used by a competitive negotiator, will be less likely to see competitive tactics used by a cooperative negotiator, will not fear cooperative tactics used by a cooperative. This loss of trust can affect not only the remainder of that negotiation, but can also compromise future negotiations with that same opponent.

Unnatural tactics employed by a less than good performer can be uncovered through a slip of the tongue, an inconsistency in either the content of the messages related, or between nonverbal and verbal behaviors. For example, a seemingly cooperative negotiator may inadvertently refer to another similar case where she "cleared out" the opponent. In another instance, the negotiator might indicate a desire to be fair as he smiles when the other negotiator on the receiving end of the tactic may sense the inconsistency and realize that the air of cooperation is merely superficial.

This recognition or uncovering of unmatched behavior to style can significantly jeopardize the potential for reaching agreement. The trickle down consequence includes jeopardizing the welfare and goals of the clients, on whose behalf the lawyers were negotiating. Ultimately, the attorney-client relationship can be impacted negatively as well if the client does not achieve what was perceived to be possible or likely through the negotiation.

A Lawyer's Guide to Effective Negotiation and Mediation, CLE edition, is the abridged version of the looseleaf edition designed for use in CLE programs. The section and form numbering from the looseleaf edition have been retained in the CLE edition.

Consistency in approach and tactic is an important component to a successful negotiation style. There are times, however, when varying or shifting one's approach can have a positive effect on the direction of the negotiation. A sudden shift in method, argument or approach, can demonstrate versatility in the negotiator's skill and shift the focus of the discussion.

A significant shift in tone, for example, can lead the other negotiator to pay closer attention to the point under discussion. The quiet, reserved negotiator who suddenly bellows with outrage will trigger more attention than one who yells throughout the discussion. Gerard I. Nierenberg, *The Art of Negotiating* (Hawthorn Books, 1968) at 112. A shift in approach can also be introduced to catch the other side off guard or to encourage a quick response. Mark K. Schoenfield and Rick Schoenfield, *Legal Negotiations: Getting Maximum Results* (McGraw–Hill, 1988) at 178–79.

In short, tactics need to be selected purposefully and exercised knowingly. Each statement or accompanying cue affects the direction and tone of the discussions. Failure to monitor the cues of others, or to proceed without awareness of one's own nonverbal messages is a road to ineffective negotiation. Final agreement terms will be arrived at as a result of the verbal exchanges and perceptions of nonverbal cues; each such message need be sent or received with a monitored accuracy.

§ 6.4 An Arsenal of Tactics

Tactics may be divided into three categories: cooperative, competitive, and yielding. Cooperative or problem-solving tactics are beneficial when the negotiators perceive a mutuality of interest. Competitive tactics reflect the negotiators' efforts at positional maneuvering. Yield tactics exhibit deference to the conduct or approach of the other negotiators and are useful mostly when there are time restraints.

The specific tactic selected will not necessarily reflect the negotiating style of the person, i.e., a competitive negotiator does not necessarily use only competitive tactics.

A Lawyer's Guide to Effective Negotiation and Mediation, CLE edition, is the abridged version of the looseleaf edition designed for use in CLE programs. The section and form numbering from the looseleaf edition have been retained in the CLE edition.

See § 6.1, *supra*. Competitive negotiators may prefer a cooperative or yielding tactic in a deliberate attempt to modify image or position posture; the cooperative negotiators may resort to competitive tactics in response to rising frustration or non-response from the other negotiator. Tactic selection, in addition to being affected by negotiator personality, will also be affected by the environment in which the negotiation takes place.

In addition to the strategic selection of a location for negotiation for the purpose of controlling the interaction (see § 3.4, *supra*), the effect of the environment itself on tactic selection should also be considered. For example, interaction conducted in a quiet restaurant or at a neutral person's office carries certain requirements of appropriate demeanor. Maintaining a certain tone of voice and expectations of proper conduct can frame the interaction. Conduct which is appropriate for one setting may not be so in another. Put differently, part of the negotiators' planning is to consider the appropriateness of particular tactics given the setting for the negotiation. The cooperative negotiator may prefer negotiating with a competitive opponent in a family oriented environment, for example, in the hope that the tactics adopted by the competitive person will be appropriate to the setting.

An important component to utilizing tactics effectively in negotiation is the largely unconscious process of face saving. This process is grounded in the need to appear capable and competent to the other negotiators and to avoid tactics that will make the other negotiator look foolish in the process. Larry L. Teply, *Legal Negotiation in a Nutshell*, (West Publishing, 1992) at p. 198.

Each negotiator depends on maintaining her status, prestige, and recognition in the eyes of the other negotiators. Where one of these components is in jeopardy, moves can be made to repair and restore that negotiator's self-esteem and status in the process. Failure to restore face through apology or some other effort to refocus the process onto positions and not personal attacks will jeopardize the progress of the process; making the effort to repair face means acknowledging the misfocus and then

A Lawyer's Guide to Effective Negotiation and Mediation, CLE edition, is the abridged version of the looseleaf edition designed for use in CLE programs. The section and form numbering from the looseleaf edition have been retained in the CLE edition.

avoiding additional judgments on the actions and motives of the other.

§ 6.5 Competitive Tactics

The following tactics are competitive in nature. Their use may trigger a like or dissimilar reaction by the other negotiator.

(1) **Threat and Argument.** These are common tools in any conflict or adversarial interaction and often reflect human nature and frustrations. In the negotiation setting, these behaviors rarely prove to be beneficial to the progress of the interaction or resolution sought by the participants.

A threat is a commitment made by a negotiator to take some action that will be detrimental to the other negotiators or their clients, unless the others comply with the set out condition or request. Donald G. Gifford, *Legal Negotiation: Theory and Applications* (West Publishing, 1989) at 143–145.

Threats should be used sparingly, if at all, in negotiation, notwithstanding the ever-present possibility of the use of threat in every negotiation; a negotiator always stands ready to walk away from the session if conditions deteriorate. Threats often elicit counter-threats which merely trigger or increase hostility between the negotiators.

A negotiator who resorts to using threats has either lost interest in the welfare of the other negotiators, assumes the others have lost interest in his welfare, or never had any concern for the others in the first place. Gerald R. Williams, *Legal Negotiation and Settlement* (West Publishing, 1983) at 55–56. Threats shift negotiation discussions away from understanding ideas and positions and onto surviving the process. They jeopardize whatever level of positive relationship exists between the negotiators. In short, threats increase the likelihood that an impasse will occur. *Id.,* at 56. See also: Fisher & Ury, *Getting to Yes* (Penguin Books, 1983) at 5.

Notes

Argument shifts the discussion away from the merits of the positions presented; it denigrates the conversation to attacks on people or conduct. Argument is a tool for achieving concessions if the receiver of the tactic is intimidated by or otherwise accepts the viewpoint of the arguer. The term argument, as used here, does not refer to the reaction of a thought out, supported and structured position.

Certainly the use of legal argument and of precedent incorporated into a rational position is quite appropriate when presented with a respectful demeanor, i.e., with respect for the other negotiators. Here, reference is made to irrational argument which degenerates into oratory; this should be avoided in negotiation.

(2) **Asymmetrical Time Pressure.** This popular tactic of the Japanese negotiator is useful when negotiating with foreign visitors. The host negotiator asks the visiting opponents for their scheduled time of departure, ostensibly to confirm flight arrangements. Then, hospitality and social events flow thereby preventing any discussion of business until shortly before the scheduled departure time.

The approach is tied to negotiation with the Japanese because of that country's strong reliance on relational trust. The Japanese will not conduct business with another person until there has been adequate interaction, rapport, and a sense of fairness. Thus, failure to reach an agreement by the time of departure may be a necessity from the Japanese viewpoint, if insufficient trust exists to permit business dealings.

From the American perspective, the use of time pressure is to force the acceptance of last minute terms. If used successfully by Americans, the visitors are forced to make a number of concessions they might not otherwise have made in order to avoid returning home without an agreement. This tactic works best when the visiting negotiators are required by their superior to return home with an agreement. Charles B. Craver, *Effective Legal Negotiation and Settlement* (Michie Company, 1986) at 130.

A Lawyer's Guide to Effective Negotiation and Mediation, CLE edition, is the abridged version of the looseleaf edition designed for use in CLE programs. The section and form numbering from the looseleaf edition have been retained in the CLE edition.

(3) **Belly-Up.** A reflection of Peter Falk's famous character, Lt. Columbo, best illustrates this negotiation tactic. The seemingly naive and out-classed negotiator appears willing to follow the lead of the other negotiator. The former negotiator encourages the latter negotiator to take the lead, make the first offer, or the first concession, on the pretense of that other persons' experience. *Id.*, at 138–40.

When employed by a skilled, experienced negotiator, the tactic is an excellent means of eliciting information disclosures and relying on the other experienced negotiator's good nature to better the position of the user. Of course, the more experienced the recipient of this tactic, the less likely they are to disclose valuable information; they understand the importance of controlling disclosure.

(4) **Bluffing.** This common and traditional tactic consists of the user's stating a position as if there were no possibility for compromise or modification of it. The intent of a bluff is to provoke a particular response or positional move by the other negotiator. This tactic carries the repercussion of possible loss of credibility of the user. It can also create suspicion in the interaction and even impact on that user's reputation for the future. Mark K. Schoenfield and Rick Schoenfield, *Legal Negotiations: Getting Maximum Results* (McGraw–Hill, 1988).

If use of bluffing is uncovered, then the other negotiators will lose whatever regard they had for the user and his statements of position.

(5) **Boulwareism.** This tactic, named after Lemuel Boulware, is more popularly called "take it or leave it." See, Lemuel Boulware, The Truth About Boulwareism (BNA, 1969). "Boulwareism" consists of stating an offer to opponents as firm and non-negotiable; the offer is neither subject to revision, nor is it open for discussion. The history of this tactic lies in an agreement of negotiator Lemuel Boulware's bypassing the Electrical Workers Union on behalf of the General Electric Company with a proposal he stated was final, unless the union could present facts he had overlooked. The National Labor Rela-

A Lawyer's Guide to Effective Negotiation and Mediation, CLE edition, is the abridged version of the looseleaf edition designed for use in CLE programs. The section and form numbering from the looseleaf edition have been retained in the CLE edition.

93

tions Board held this to be an unfair labor practice. Boulware argued that both parties fully understood what the final settlement would be. He described all of the intervening bargaining discussion as nothing more than an expensive fraud.

His philosophy underscores this "best offer first" tactic as it is understood today. This tactic should be used only by someone of perceived or actual significant power and authority who will actually carry out the promise *not* to compromise. A common and anticipated response to this tactic is impasse.

In reality, few people use this tactic because it encourages impasse by blocking the give-and-take exchange most negotiators need to experience psychologically. Moreover, while many people believe they will not shift from a position, a counteroffer that comes quite close to the firmly stated position will appear to be attractive. For example, would a take it or leave it demand of $1,000 fail in the event of an offer of $990? From a competitive viewpoint, perhaps. However, the establishment of sound principle, including the exhaustion of available funds, may lead to a reconsideration and acceptance.

(6) **Brer Rabbit, or "Anything but that."** The story of Brer Rabbit involves a fox contemplating the fate of a rabbit he traps. The rabbit begs for any fate except that he pleads not to be thrown into the brier-patch; in reality, the brier-patch is precisely the fate desired by the rabbit. Following repeated requests, the fox decides to do just what the rabbit says he does *not* want.

In negotiation, a negotiator may end up with what she says she doesn't want, whether or not she actually wants it. Charles B. Craver, *Effective Legal Negotiation and Settlement* (Michie Company, 1986) at 132–33. This technique suggests that receiving an offer of value may better be responded to as though the offer is of little value. If the offerer senses a need for something, she may decide to limit additional concessions or offers, or view meeting that one need as sufficient concession.

A Lawyer's Guide to Effective Negotiation and Mediation, CLE edition, is the abridged version of the looseleaf edition designed for use in CLE programs. The section and form numbering from the looseleaf edition have been retained in the CLE edition.

(7) **Crossroads or Tangled Webs.** The negotiator introduces several elements into the negotiation in order to catch the opponent in a cross-fire. In effect, the recipient of the tactic has difficulty discerning which issues are important to the opponent, at least initially.

Concessions are made by the user of this tactic on insignificant elements, which serve to bolster that negotiator's ability to win the more important elements in conflict. Gerard I. Nierenberg, *The Art of Negotiating* (Hawthorn Books, 1968) at 117–18. Recipients of this tactic will often feel pressure to make counter concessions if only to achieve balance.

(8) **Disassociation.** This tactic calls attention to the undesirable associations of the opponent. Often times, a negotiator will hold fast to a demand or position because it becomes tied to a certain meaning or value. Certainly people are resistant to persuasion or any attempt to modify their attitudes and values.

Disassociation represents an attempt, not to change an attitude, but to break the connection between the thing desired and its psychological or attitudinal anchor. Put differently, the goal is to break the psychological connection between perceived interests and what is required to meet them.

(9) **Fait Accompli.** The negotiator takes an action without consulting the other side. This tactic should be employed with caution. It necessitates serious reflection by the user for the possible consequences of taking any such action. Once an action is taken, the user can only hope for concurrence or acquiescence by the opponent. It should be apparent that negative responses, such as impasse, need to be anticipated. *Id.,* at 113.

(10) **Feigning.** The negotiator appears to shift his position in one direction in order to divert attention away from the real goal or object. For example, the user may create the false impression that he needs more information on an issue than he actually does not need.

The recipient may comply with the request, or at least assume that the request was a sincere one. The re-

A Lawyer's Guide to Effective Negotiation and Mediation, CLE edition, is the abridged version of the looseleaf edition designed for use in CLE programs. The section and form numbering from the looseleaf edition have been retained in the CLE edition.

sult may be a concession hoped for in another area by the user of the tactic. *Id.,* at 116.

(11) **Limits.** This tactic creates pressure in the negotiation by imposing limitations on time, the number of issues to be discussed, or the location for the negotiation. This power ploy may trigger compliance, anger or impasse. *Id.,* at 115–16. Use of this tactic should be proceeded by a consideration of negotiation style.

Competitive negotiators will unlikely be phased by the pressure; they ignore deadlines. Ineffective cooperative negotiators are most likely candidates to begin making concessions in response to the tactic.

(12) **Media or Community Pressure.** This tactic is available essentially in high profile matters. The user's statement of position may include the possibility of contacting media or otherwise igniting community pressure. If public pressure is not desired by the recipient, then the use of this tactic can be quite strong and persuasive. Mark K. Schoenfeld and Rick Schoenfeld, *Legal Negotiations: Getting Maximum Results* (McGraw–Hill, 1988).

(13) **Mutt and Jeff, or "Good Cop/Bad Cop."** This tactic is available for use by a negotiating team. One member of the negotiating team appears to be cooperative (willing to compromise) while the other presents an image of being stubborn and uncompromising. The "good cop" thanks the opponent for being cooperative and helping the negotiation to progress.

For example, "you are really being fair in your position and approach and I appreciate it . . ." then the ploy takes effect. ". . . However, my boss just won't accept these terms. I see the fairness in them, but I really need your help in creating terms that my boss can accept." The opponent who accepts this statement may try to better the position in the spirit of cooperation.

The tactic can be modified for use by a negotiator who works alone; the negotiator simply references the absent client or team member who is painted to be the stubborn, ungiving person. Charles B. Craver, *Effective Legal Negotiation and Settlement* (Michie Company, 1986)

A Lawyer's Guide to Effective Negotiation and Mediation, CLE edition, is the abridged version of the looseleaf edition designed for use in CLE programs. The section and form numbering from the looseleaf edition have been retained in the CLE edition.

96

at 134–36. Essentially, one team member is disliked while the charm and good nature of the other serves to win over the favor of the opponent.

(14) **Limited Authority.** The negotiator claims to have only a limited amount or level of authority which may readily be offered. At any time the interaction becomes complicated or difficult, the user states that she needs to go back to the person with authority for approval. The break in the interaction permits thinking time for the user of the tactic and can cause frustration in the other negotiator.

If the statement of limited authority is true, then the recipient may best be advised to consider working within the stated limits if time is of the essence. If the statement is not true, i.e., the negotiator can go further in an offer, then the recipient is being tested for her response to pressure.

The recipient who is uncertain of the validity of the comment is best urged to provide some contact time for the user of the tactic, so long as there is no pending deadline. To do otherwise could lead to compromise in position when one is not necessary.

(15) **Reversal.** The negotiator takes the offensive on an issue newly raised for discussion, after he has otherwise been on the defensive for all previously discussed issues. Gerard I. Nierenberg, *The Art of Negotiating* (Hawthorn Books, 1968) at 115. Reversal often confuses the recipient because the tactic shifts the control or domination in the discussion.

(16) **Demonstrate Commitment.** It is sometimes difficult for the cooperative negotiator to say "no" to a proposal, or for any negotiator to convince a competitive person that "no" to an offer means "no." This tactic attempts to convince the opposition of the seriousness of one's resolve.

Means of demonstrating commitment to a position include physically turning one's back on the opponent, or packing up one's file to signal an intent to leave the session. In one case, a negotiator reportedly kept a bright-

A Lawyer's Guide to Effective Negotiation and Mediation, CLE edition, is the abridged version of the looseleaf edition designed for use in CLE programs. The section and form numbering from the looseleaf edition have been retained in the CLE edition.

97

colored card and thick marker in his pocket. When necessary, he would remove the card from his pocket, write "NEVER!" on it in big, bold letters, and show it to the opposition. It may take some time, but the other side should eventually get the idea. H. William Koch, Jr., *Negotiator's Factomatic* (Prentice Hall, 1988) at 61–62.

§ 6.6 Cooperative Tactics

Users of cooperative tactics seek to be problem solvers; their efforts are often greeted with acceptance by a cooperative negotiator. The competitive negotiator will never quite trust the good intent of the user. Thus, caution should be exercised by a user of cooperative tactics to insure a competitive recipient doesn't manipulate the tactic into a tool for concessions. Among the cooperative tactics available to the negotiator are:

(1) **Association.** The negotiator attempts to benefit her position by associating it to the objectives or ideals of the other side. The user of this tactic leads the other negotiators toward seeing the value of a presented proposal as the means to meeting their own needs.

For example, contractors who are under contract to complete a sandblasting and painting project on a concrete building fall behind, unable to complete the project within the required time period. While the owners of the building have several reasons for demanding completion regardless of the overtime required, the contractors suggest waiting until Spring to complete the work.

Seemingly, an impossible position, the contractors may fare well by pointing out the significant possibility that a paint job completed prior to that time may fade and fail to hold up. The delay until Spring acknowledging that no one is happy about the delay, will mean a better guarantee of lasting workmanship. Based on a real circumstance, this instance of association between task and the building owners' fundamental interests proved to be successful.

(2) **Flexibility.** The negotiator expresses a willingness "to look again" at an issue which had been closed

A Lawyer's Guide to Effective Negotiation and Mediation, CLE edition, is the abridged version of the looseleaf edition designed for use in CLE programs. The section and form numbering from the looseleaf edition have been retained in the CLE edition.

98

earlier in the discussion. Flexibility does not require concession. Rather, it affords the other negotiators an opportunity to break out of a deadlock. Any negotiator may come to see the need for a concession or compromise. Donald G. Gifford, *Legal Negotiation: Theory and Applications* (West Publishing, 1989) at 154.

(3) **Logrolling.** Prescribed as a tool to break an impasse, the negotiator identifies everyone's concerns relative to their importance. Lesser concerns are subordinated or conceded to higher ones in an effort to encourage a "high joint benefit." This tactic is difficult to employ when other negotiating styles are strictly competitive. *Id.,* at 170. The competitive negotiator views every concession as a sign of weakness; she continues to expect more to be conceded by the opponent.

(4) **Participation ("Me too").** The negotiator demonstrates what other people have gotten in similar circumstances, followed by an argument for equity seeking similar treatment. The tactic assumes that a degree of fairness underlies the discussion. Gerard I. Nierenberg, *The Art of Negotiating* (Hawthorn Books, 1968) at 116.

(5) **Romancing.** Like participation, romancing involves demonstrating similarities between the matter at hand and others like it. Here, however, the negotiator emphasizes the importance of "joining the bandwagon" or staying a step ahead, to insure achieving terms as viable and effective as in the past cases.

The tactic is useful in transactional negotiations where current deals reflect the past and future deals look to the present. This tactic is not as useful in personal injury negotiations where each client matter is deemed unique and distinguishable. H. William Koch, Jr., *Negotiator's Factomatic* (Prentice Hall, 1988) at § 6–1.

(6) **Cutting the Salami.** Matyas Rakosi, General Secretary of the Hungarian Communist Party, is credited with naming this tactic. The negotiator recognizes that if she wants something belonging to the opponent, it is better sought slice by slice, rather than all at once. Gerard I. Nierenberg, *The Art of Negotiating* (Hawthorn Books,

A Lawyer's Guide to Effective Negotiation and Mediation, CLE edition, is the abridged version of the looseleaf edition designed for use in CLE programs. The section and form numbering from the looseleaf edition have been retained in the CLE edition.

99

1968) at 120–1. Similarly, concessions are better requested in small doses as well. It is less painful psychologically to conduct bargaining point by point than to give up too much at once. Efforts to obtain the "whole salami" in one demand make recovery a likely impossibility.

(7) **Changing Viewpoint.** The negotiator agrees to look at the issues in conflict from a different perspective, or to re-evaluate the interests underlying the presented position. Gerard I. Nierenberg, *The Art of Negotiating* (Hawthorn Books, 1973) at 174–76.

(8) **Splitting the Difference.** A popular means to achieving agreement near the end of a negotiation, this tactic requires an exchange of concessions. The negotiators agree to split equally any remaining difference, usually monetary, which is blocking agreement. This tactic is rarely used except as a final agreement-achieving effort, where it becomes a popular device. Charles B. Craver, *Effective Legal Negotiation and Settlement* (Michie Company, 1986) at 142–43.

Negotiators should view this tactic to be no more than one of the many tactics available to them. Many negotiators believe that a splitting of the difference is either required or expected as a component of professional responsibility. However, when principle or need requires it, a negotiator should not fear rejecting the tactic as an option in favor of some other means of resolution.

For example, when negotiators are within a close distance between offer and demand, one will often say, "Hey, meet me half way." It seems perfectly logical that a distance of $500 would be shared by a reduction in demand of $250 and an increase in offer of $250. There may, however, be good reason not to evenly split the difference, such as lack of funds or a commitment to a position which has a principle to support it.

§ 6.7 Yielding Tactics

At tense or other difficult moments, a negotiator may wish to yield or otherwise withdraw from the conflict, if only momentarily. Yielding tactics include:

A Lawyer's Guide to Effective Negotiation and Mediation, CLE edition, is the abridged version of the looseleaf edition designed for use in CLE programs. The section and form numbering from the looseleaf edition have been retained in the CLE edition.

(1) **Apparent Withdrawal.** The negotiator, claiming a problem exists such as the appearance of unfairness, requests a break or delay in the proceeding. This form of disrupting the proceedings may trigger defensiveness or hostility from others. One should not falsely claim the existence of unfairness or problem.

If, on the other hand, there is an appearance of inappropriate conduct, then the break provides an opportunity for the negotiators to reflect upon and shift their presentation style once the negotiation resumes. Calling a "temporary halt" to the negotiation is also useful when the interaction is perceived to be heading in a destructive or otherwise non-progressive direction. The tactic is of value when one or more negotiators is hostile or out of control. A break provides the negotiators with an opportunity to assess new information, reassess tactics, or get refreshed. Donald G. Gifford, *Legal Negotiation: Theory and Applications* (West Publishing, 1989) at 156.

(2) **Bland Withdrawal.** The negotiator acknowledges the concerns or problems presented by the other side with a sense of nonchalance; this approach serves to disarm the opponent and avoids the need for other defensive tactics. Gerard I. Nierenberg, *The Art of Negotiating* (Hawthorn Books, 1968) at 113.

These tactics are designed to disrupt a negative flow of interaction. Employing moments of reflection or refreshment can shift a negative negotiation to a successful experience, so long as each negotiator reacts appropriately to the yielding tactic.

A competitive negotiator may remain unaffected by yielding and simply resume the harmful conduct. When such is the case, the user of yielding needs to decide whether she can continue to explore a fair settlement. The essential component is recognizing the need to handle a tactic of confrontation.

*

A Lawyer's Guide to Effective Negotiation and Mediation, CLE edition, is the abridged version of the looseleaf edition designed for use in CLE programs. The section and form numbering from the looseleaf edition have been retained in the CLE edition.

BOOK TWO. MEDIATION—THE ROAD TO RESOLUTION

Chapter 7

INTRODUCTION TO MEDIATION

Table of Sections

WESTLAW Electronic Research

See WESTLAW Electronic Research Guide preceding the Summary of Contents.

Notes

§ 7.1   Role of ADR—The Perspective of the Legal System

Current litigation practice is costly and, in most urban jurisdictions, inefficient. As such, it has become a problematic vehicle of resolution for most disputes. The heavy backlog in many jurisdiction's civil courts currently requires many years for a case to reach its courtroom resolution. In reality, few cases ever reach trial and verdict; those matters that do reach the trial stage are most often settled during the proceedings prior to verdict.

There are several factors which lead to the disposition of lawsuits through a settlement. These include the general distaste that the courtroom has for many litigants; they are uncertain of what the future will hold. James W. Jeans, *Trial Advocacy* (West Publishing, 1975) at 426. In addition, trial is expensive and produces significant risk of psychological and social discomfort. The complexity of legal cases and issues in corporate settings, for example,

---

A Lawyer's Guide to Effective Negotiation and Mediation, CLE edition, is the abridged version of the looseleaf edition designed for use in CLE programs. The section and form numbering from the looseleaf edition have been retained in the CLE edition.

present delicate concerns of creating resolution while maintaining interpersonal relationships between the parties who may continue with professional relations.

In addition to the entangled process of the law, the legal system is also incomprehensible to anyone but lawyers. Our trial system has been described as a "sudden regression to childhood, where you can understand neither the procedures nor the language, where your attorney assumes the role of a parent and you become the dependent child, and where the judge looms as a menacing authority figure, empowered to divest you of property or liberty." Peter Lovenheim, *Mediate, Don't Litigate: How to Resolve Disputes Quickly, Privately and Inexpensively without Going to Court* (McGraw–Hill, 1989) at 14.

Calls for systemic reform have come from the highest level of the legal system. Former Chief Justice Warren Burger, an ardent supporter of "alternative dispute resolution" (ADR) wrote:

> The notion that ordinary people want black-robed judges and well dressed lawyers and fine courtrooms as settings to resolve their disputes is not correct. People with problems, like people with pains, want relief, and they want it as quickly and inexpensively as possible.

> *The 1985 Chief Justice Earl Warren Conference on Advocacy: Dispute Resolution Devices in a Democratic Society* (Roscoe Pound—American Trial Lawyers Foundation, 1985).

Early efforts in the development of non-trial dispute resolution were initiated at an American Bar Association conference on dispute resolution techniques held in 1977 at Columbia University. The conference helped publicize and, in some views, legitimatize the many forms of ADR, most of which include a third party to facilitate the process. As a result, the traditional ADR methods of arbitration and mediation have been supplemented by modern reforms including pretrial diversion, advisory sentencing panels, victim assistance and restitution programs.

A Lawyer's Guide to Effective Negotiation and Mediation, CLE edition, is the abridged version of the looseleaf edition designed for use in CLE programs. The section and form numbering from the looseleaf edition have been retained in the CLE edition.

The growth of alternative dispute resolution has occurred as a part of the so-called "transformational" movement of the 1970's. This underlying social movement sought to change the basic societal underpinnings of the legal system, through:

(A) Change created by consensus (vs. imposed on society);

(B) Individually-based service (vs. institutional application);

(C) Search for win-win solutions (vs. a win-lose result);

(D) Incorporation of intuitive-based processes (vs. logic or rational-based processes); and

(E) Decentralization of decision making power (vs. centralization).

Marilyn Ferguson, *The Aquarian Conspiracy* (J.P. Tarcher, 1980).

The legal and societal movements led to a coalition of professionals to join together in the creation of a new field and profession: "the problem solver." Numbering among those creating the field were lawyers, psychologists, politicians, and administrators.

The value of ADR to the improvement of the legal system itself and likely the motive behind the current interest in alternative dispute resolution include:

(1) It saves time and money;

(2) It rescues a vastly overburdened judicial system;

(3) It is more responsive to the unique problems presented by each case;

(4) It can better address the human values often involved in litigation; and

(5) It protects the image of the legal profession as the means toward resolution.

The real issue seems to be whether those who are urged to seek out and utilize ADR within the legal profession are capable of being effective in the process given the

---

A Lawyer's Guide to Effective Negotiation and Mediation, CLE edition, is the abridged version of the looseleaf edition designed for use in CLE programs. The section and form numbering from the looseleaf edition have been retained in the CLE edition.

Notes

adversarial training and viewpoints that mark the strategies employed primarily in the legal process.

The training and makeup of the American lawyer may not be reflective of a person suited for a role in the alternative dispute resolution methods. Leonard Riskin, "Mediation and Lawyers," 43 Ohio St.L.J. 29, 1982. Every form of dispute resolution requires, by definition, cooperation and individualization. Legally trained advocates of ADR point to the importance of proper training prior to becoming a practitioner of ADR.

In response to traditional legal training which did not emphasize cooperative dispute resolution, but rather relied on the teaching of adversarial skills, there has been a recent growth in the study and teaching of ADR in law schools, other post-graduate programs and continuing legal education presentations throughout the country. There are numerous training sessions and conferences open to all people with an interest in resolving disputes outside the courtroom. The legal system itself seems greatly committed to the value and potential of ADR as an important arm of the legal process.

In many cases, practitioners receive certification for completion of extensive coursework and practicum experience. They argue that such training is important prior to holding oneself out as capable in practicing ADR. In today's era of lawyers seeking alternative careers to the traditional practice of law, ADR has become an outlet for a growing number of young professionals who wish to pursue conflict resolving, rather than conflict enhancing, careers.

Meetings of people in conflict have great potential for displays of emotion and lapses of logic. As such, the practitioner of ADR needs to be capable of handling a host of human dynamics and interactions.

§ 7.2 Types of Conflict Resolution—In General

There are a variety of forms which the exercise of alternative dispute resolution through a third party can take. Certainly, the lawyers and parties exercise their

A Lawyer's Guide to Effective Negotiation and Mediation, CLE edition, is the abridged version of the looseleaf edition designed for use in CLE programs. The section and form numbering from the looseleaf edition have been retained in the CLE edition.

106

negotiation skills as a tool and means of resolving disputes through the non-litigation dispute resolution mechanisms.

The table which follows sets out the fundamental differences between the common forms of third party ADR. The methods are discussed in greater depth thereafter.

DISPUTE RESOLUTION TABLE

	Adjudication	Arbitration	Med–Arb	Mediation	Negotiation
Flexibility	Low	Low	Moderate	High	Very High
Formality	Very formal and structured	Somewhat formal but less structured	Somewhat less formal and structured	Usually informal with little structure	Usually informal with little structure
Coercion	High	High-little	High-none	Some-none	Usually none
Binding	Yes, but may be appealed	Yes,* but may be appealed on limited grounds	Yes,* but may be appealed on limited grounds	Only if agreement is an enforceable contract	Only if agreement is an enforceable contract
Third Party Participation	High	High	High	Some	N/A (No Third Party)
Decision by	Third Party	Third Party	Third Party as last resort only	Parties (with help from Third Party)	Parties Only
Visibility	Public	Private (unless review sought)	Private (unless review sought)	Private	Private

* Arbitration and the arbitration option of Med–Arb can also be non-binding.

	Mini-trial	Private Judging	Fact-finding	Conciliation/ Facilitation	Ombudsman
Flexibility	Some	More than standard Adj.	High	Very High	Some
Formality	Less than standard Adj. but still somewhat formal	Less than standard Adj. but still somewhat formal	Informal	Very informal	Informal
Coercion	Some	Some	None	None	None
Binding	Only if in prior agreement	Yes, but may be appealed	No, but results may be admissible in Adj.	No	No
Third Party Participation	Varies: Some-little	High	High or none (if by parties only)	Little	High
Decision by	Parties (Third Party might make suggestions)	Third Party	Limited decision by Third Party or Parties (if joint process)	Parties	Advisory decision by Third Party
Visibility	Private	Private	Private (can be public if issue Adj. later)	Private	Private

---

A Lawyer's Guide to Effective Negotiation and Mediation, CLE edition, is the abridged version of the looseleaf edition designed for use in CLE programs. The section and form numbering from the looseleaf edition have been retained in the CLE edition.

Notes

§ 7.15 Is Mediation the Best Method of ADR?

The most effective and efficient way to resolve a dispute is for the parties to create their own solution through the exercise of negotiation skills. The consistent problem with negotiation is that disputes are not often resolved to the satisfaction of the parties, if they are resolved at all.

While third party intervention into a dispute requires a person who has no real substantive interest in or prior working knowledge of the conflict, mediation nevertheless offers a better chance for resolution than does strictly adversarial negotiation.

Skilled mediators will intervene only as much as they need to in order to resolve the dispute. The mediator's role can range from a strong authoritarian who exerts control over the interaction to the weak and almost nonexistent mediator. Of course, mediators do not dictate solutions like an arbitrator does, but the distinctions between the two can sometimes become blurred.

A strong and controlling mediator might suggest solutions or push the parties toward a specific resolution deemed to be advantageous to all sides. Howard Raiffa, "Mediation of Conflicts," 12 Amer.Behav.Sci., Dec. 1983, at 195. Regardless of the particular mediator's style, the common factor in all mediation is that, with the exercise of negotiation skills, the parties must reach their own solution or there will be no solution reached through the process.

The power of mediation lies in the creation of the solution by the parties. This component makes mediation superior to both litigation and even arbitration. If the final agreement is one truly reached by a "meeting of the minds," then its enforcement will not be a matter of concern. The win/lose nature of litigation often means that securing compliance with a resolution (judgment) frequently takes longer than the process itself.

Mediation makes it possible for parties to compromise without losing face or appearing weak. They can confide in the mediator in private caucus and rely on the

---

A Lawyer's Guide to Effective Negotiation and Mediation, CLE edition, is the abridged version of the looseleaf edition designed for use in CLE programs. The section and form numbering from the looseleaf edition have been retained in the CLE edition.

mediator's maintaining confidence. In addition, a cooperative atmosphere to foster creativity between the parties in problem resolution is the goal of the mediator. The parties are enabled to create a win/win situation with third party mediator assistance.

Unfortunately, while mediation enhances the settlement process, it does not guarantee settlement. Litigation, arbitration, and mediation/arbitration all ensure that the conflict will be resolved through the process, one way or another. Of course, the resolutions reached through these other means are more likely seen as systemic impositions.

In most cases, parties see the advantage over other methods of resolving their own disputes through mutual agreement. It often takes the keen skill of the mediator to have the parties shed their egos and uncover the point of agreement.

Mediation will likely prove to be valuable whether used prior to or after other forms of dispute resolution because of its nature. Since resolution in mediation emerges from the parties, there is rarely reason not to attempt the process. An exception may be that the case at hand is not ripe for mediation, but the form also includes this component for the lawyer to evaluate.

§ 7.16 Mediator—Defined

The goal of a mediator is to help the parties in dispute reach a settlement. The mediator uses an arsenal of communication and procedural skills to help the parties reach a settlement. The mediator's determination of *when* to intervene is more important than *how* he chooses to intervene; timing can be critical. Sometimes parties refuse to submit their case to mediation until they have reached an impasse. Unfortunately, in some cases, the point of impasse is often too late and amicable agreement is foreclosed.

Finding a proper time for mediation is a decision often not involving the mediator. The mediator needs to consider the case-relevant history which has occurred

---

A Lawyer's Guide to Effective Negotiation and Mediation, CLE edition, is the abridged version of the looseleaf edition designed for use in CLE programs. The section and form numbering from the looseleaf edition have been retained in the CLE edition.

Notes

prior to the mediation. The emotions and dynamics require the mediator to seek balance in the interaction between the parties and their dispute. The techniques and communication skills exercised during the process play a key role in the effectiveness of the mediator. Not every lawyer's personality is suited to being an effective mediator.

One well-respected mediator, William Simkin, offers, with underlying humor, the following qualities of the effective mediator:

(1) The patience of Job;

(2) The sincerity and bulldog characteristics of the English;

(3) The wit of the Irish;

(4) The physical endurance of a marathon runner;

(5) The broken-field dodging ability of a halfback;

(6) The guile of Machiavelli;

(7) The personality probing skills of a good psychiatrist;

(8) The confidence-retaining characteristics of a mute;

(9) The hide of a rhinoceros; and

(10) The wisdom of Solomon.

In a more serious vein, Simkin adds:

(11) Demonstrated integrity and impartiality;

(12) A basic knowledge of and belief in the collective bargaining process;

(13) Firm faith in volunteering, in contrast to dictation;

(14) A fundamental belief in human values and potentials, tempered by the ability to assess personal weakness as well as strengths;

(15) A hard-nosed ability to analyze what is available, in contrast to what may be desirable; and

(16) Sufficient personal drive and ego, qualified by a willingness to be self-effacing.

A Lawyer's Guide to Effective Negotiation and Mediation, CLE edition, is the abridged version of the looseleaf edition designed for use in CLE programs. The section and form numbering from the looseleaf edition have been retained in the CLE edition.

Howard Raiffa, "Mediation of Conflicts," 12 Amer. Behav.Sci., Dec. 1983, at 209.

§ 7.17 Mediator—Background

Today, effective mediators come from a variety of backgrounds and education. In the early days of mediation, experience in the particular area of the law in which the mediation was to be conducted was considered the mediator's most important qualification. It was assumed that the skills of mediation would be acquired through practice.

Education was not considered to be as important as experience. For example, about one third of the mediators of the Federal Mediation and Conciliation Service (FMCS), responsible for handling labor disputes, had no education above the high school level; nearly ten percent of the mediators had not finished high school and only about fifteen percent of the FMCS mediators had graduate degrees. William Simkin and Nicholas Fiandis, *Mediation and the Dynamics of Collective Bargaining* (BNA, 1986) at 46. The mediators did, however, have extensive experience in labor dispute resolution, either as a mediator or as a party representative. *Id.* at 48.

The recent explosion of interest in ADR has resulted in the field becoming a profession. As a consequence, the prevailing view is that an extensive formal education is now critical to one's success as a mediator. Of course, many lawyers believe that being a lawyer, an academician, or even a judge, is a prerequisite to being a mediator.

Certainly, an extensive battery of theoretical skills is necessary to effective mediation. The mediator's abilities should, for example, include the ability to "model the dynamic interactive events" of a contingent solution to a dispute. Howard Raiffa, "Mediation of Conflicts," 12 Amer.Behav.Sci., Dec. 1983, at 197.

Whatever educational training a mediator pursues should include skill development in analyzing issues and problems. Anything that gives the mediator insight into

Notes

human thought and nature is helpful. Degrees in communication, psychology, sociology, anthropology, and most other social sciences provide such a background. The ability to think creatively is also important.

Perhaps the ties to tradition inherent in legal training present a barrier to the frame of mind necessary for the mediator. However, lawyers who have experience creating settlement agreements and innovative legal theories may very well possess the analytical potential for serving as a mediator.

Certainly, experience in the specific area of law for which one wishes to serve as a mediator goes a long way to insuring that legal issues are understood and that the mediation is not impeded due to a lack of substantive knowledge. The parties find the process easier for themselves if they do not have to explain the terminology or nuances of the relevant facts and legal issues to the mediator.

Conversely, a mediator who believes that additional information is necessary prior to continuing the process should not hesitate to seek such information from the parties or an outside source. This may entail a delay in the mediation, but such is better than proceeding without the necessary substantive background.

Chapter 9

THE PROCESS OF MEDIATION

Table of Sections

WESTLAW Electronic Research

See WESTLAW Electronic Research Guide preceding the Summary of Contents.

Notes

§ 9.1   The Participants

The participants in the mediation process include, the disputing parties, their counsel, and the mediator. In addition, any other non-interested third party that is included at the request of the mediator or the interested parties may attend, subject to agreement by the others in attendance.

A party in the mediation is a person, representing themselves or an entity such as a corporation, with an identifiable interest in the dispute at hand. What or who constitutes a party in mediation is not as easy a question as it might appear.

Ordinarily, there are two parties in a mediation, but the number of disputants can be many more than two. For example, environmental disputes can bring a dozen or more parties to the mediation. In addition, a party may be only one person or could consist of a group or class of people, such as a national union. In its broadest sense, a

A Lawyer's Guide to Effective Negotiation and Mediation, CLE edition, is the abridged version of the looseleaf edition designed for use in CLE programs. The section and form numbering from the looseleaf edition have been retained in the CLE edition.

party in an environmental dispute, for example, could be the public at large.

The roles of the parties in a mediation can vary with the issues to be negotiated in and the posture of the case. Given the vast number of personalities that can present themselves as a party, it becomes impossible to generalize about mediation goals or expected roles that will be enacted by the parties. One assumption seems appropriate: the goal of each party is to reach a settlement. Absent this mindset, there is little purpose in pursuing the process of mediation.

The initial part of every mediation is an orientation which establishes the demeanor and roles of each party, their lawyers and the mediator. See § 9.7, *infra*. This consideration is important both for how the parties will interact between themselves and with the mediator. The parties may be prepared to relate their account of events, but may not have thought through the implications and consequences of the matter as a whole.

For example, parties do not often have a thorough analysis of the problem or their adversary's needs in their minds prior to the mediation. In fact, given the emotional ties a party can have to the substance of the matter, an extensive analysis can become self-defeating.

Parties can become defensive of their own evaluation or analysis in the mediation; they may also expect the other side to present a perspective and conduct based in rationality. Howard Raifa, "Mediation of Conflict," 12 Amer.Behav.Sci. 195 (Dec., 1983) at 201. Failure to meet expectations can lead to difficulties in carrying through the process.

Parties are sometimes resistant to mediation because of the seemingly inherent conflict in the process. Mediation, by definition, incorporates competition represented by the differences between party positions. Simultaneously, the process relies on the cooperation of the parties to create an acceptable agreement between them.

Thus, mediation requires and relies upon the parties cooperating towards settlement. Failure to offer conces-

A Lawyer's Guide to Effective Negotiation and Mediation, CLE edition, is the abridged version of the looseleaf edition designed for use in CLE programs. The section and form numbering from the looseleaf edition have been retained in the CLE edition.

114

sions will freeze the parties in their initial positions and preclude agreement. In fact, many parties perceive the mediator's objective to be one of forcing the parties to make concessions. Co-existing with the need for cooperation and an inherent presence of competition is the foundation of mediation.

These seemingly contradictory components of mediation create a tension in the process that needs to be alleviated by the mediator during the initial orientation to the process. Parties need to understand and realize that the process recognizes both cooperation and competition. The mediator needs to create balance in the mediation so that neither party steamrolls the other to agreement.

In the end, mediation can only be successful if the settlement considers and reflects the interests and meets the needs of the parties. A mediator can take very few steps to protect one party's interests before appearing to be partial. Nothing is as important to the mediation process as the mediator's image of impartiality. Thus, the competitive component of negotiation in the process needs to resolve itself under the guidance of the mediator and with a recognition that the parties will negotiate for their own interests throughout the process.

Not every party is a willing participant in mediation. Many courts now have mandatory referral programs that send potential litigants into the forum of resolution, sometimes against their desires. Other parties are forced into mediation by contractual provisions and still others find themselves subjected to mediation as the best alternative to the prospect of complex, time consuming, and costly litigation.

Admittedly, considerable resistance comes from parties who are simply unfamiliar with mediation. Uninformed persons customarily prefer more familiar routes to mediators, even though the alternatives are perceived to be inadequate. Kenneth Feinberg, "Mediation—A Preferred Method of Dispute Resolution," 16 Pepperdine L.Rev. s5 at s20 –s21 (1989) (WESTLAW: PEPLR database, **ci(16 +5 s5)**). Candidly, even attorneys can be resis-

A Lawyer's Guide to Effective Negotiation and Mediation, CLE edition, is the abridged version of the looseleaf edition designed for use in CLE programs. The section and form numbering from the looseleaf edition have been retained in the CLE edition.

tent to the process because they are traditionally educated to view litigation as the paramount form of dispute resolution.

After all, dispute resolution is contrary to the goal of many lawyers who seek increased billing. In reality, lower legal fees are the goal of clients, but billable hours may be the only source of income for many of the lawyers who represent them. Education is the best remedy for this blockage; a satisfied client will bring return business to the lawyer who resolves matters efficiently and cost effectively.

§ 9.6 The Mediation Process—In General

The mediator needs to monitor the stages of mediation as a means of measuring the progress and direction of the interaction. The nature of the conflict and the personalities of the disputants affects the manner in which a mediation progresses; therefore, each mediation moves through a basic progression of stages, though at different rates and ways. By following a standard format and setting out the process to the parties, even the experienced mediator has a point of return for handling the mediation mechanism should something go wrong in the process.

There are two categories of mediator conduct: contingent actions and non-contingent actions. Contingent actions are "mediation tactics" that represent a tactical response to the situation. Caucusing with each party is an example of a contingent action. Non-contingent actions are taken regardless of the circumstances, as they reflect the functions the mediator performs in every mediation as part of the "mediation process."

The selection of particular contingent and non-contingent actions is triggered by the circumstances in the mediation and the style of the mediator. Every mediation is different in some way, so the certainty of success of any particular action is not guaranteed. Mediators can emphasize any particular action they feel will assist the interaction. Other actions can be deemphasized or avoided. For example, permitting a party to vent anger may progress one mediation but serve to block another. Media-

A Lawyer's Guide to Effective Negotiation and Mediation, CLE edition, is the abridged version of the looseleaf edition designed for use in CLE programs. The section and form numbering from the looseleaf edition have been retained in the CLE edition.

tors clearly need good judgement and an ability to read the status of the interaction.

§ 9.7 Beginning the Session

The beginning of the mediation sets the tone for the rest of the process. The mediator should seek to establish a positive attitude, create a cooperative atmosphere, and reinforce commitment to the process. There are several goals that the mediator's opening statement should accomplish:

- Introducing the mediator and (if necessary) the parties;
- Educating the parties about the process;
- Explaining the ground rules, logistics and procedures; and
- Confirming the mediator's impartiality and confidentiality.

This opening statement should be clear and concise. The mediator should avoid the use of jargon and be aware that this introduction will set the pace for the interaction; it should not appear to or be perceived to be "rushed" by the parties. First, the mediator introduces himself and the parties to each other. In so doing, the mediator should also check for any potential conflicts of interest between himself and the parties.

If there is any question regarding the impartiality of the mediator, then immediate withdrawal by the mediator is strongly recommended, unless the party that would be adversely affected unequivocally consents to continuing. Any decision reached with the assistance of a mediator who is perceived to be less than impartial can always be subject to challenge or resentment.

The mediator can also uncover whether any of the parties have prior experience with mediation. If the parties and the mediator are previously acquainted, and assuming there is no conflict, or if the parties have experience with mediation, then this initial orientation may be shortened.

If any of the parties reveal that they have participated in a prior mediation, the mediator should probe for residual feelings about the process. Most parties, especially those willing enough to engage in mediation again, will likely have a positive outlook about the process; this will help to set a positive tone. However, should a party have a negative outlook, the mediator should invest some time to uncover the underlying occurrences or reasons for the lack of success. If possible, the mediator should show how this particular mediation can be different.

There are several reasons to educate the parties about the process of mediation: (1) to minimize their potential surprise, misunderstanding, and misconceptions about the process; (2) to define and clarify the roles of the parties and the mediator; and (3) to gain feedback from the parties on their feelings about the process.

This educational effort should reference:

- The mediation procedure as a whole, broken down into stages, if necessary for inexperienced parties;
- The basic ground rules of the process, and any specific rules of the particular mediation;
- The procedures for gathering;
- How separate party caucuses will be handled;
- The requirement that the parties must be the ones to reach the agreement, as it will not be imposed upon them by the mediator; and
- The possible forms of settlement and what the mediator's participation in drafting that agreement can be.

The experience and sophistication of the parties will reflect the necessary level of explanation. Parties unfamiliar with mediation will need a deeper explanation of the basics of the process; those who are more sophisticated in the process, such as attorneys and business professionals, may need only a review of the intricacies and idiosyncracies of the process.

A Lawyer's Guide to Effective Negotiation and Mediation, CLE edition, is the abridged version of the looseleaf edition designed for use in CLE programs. The section and form numbering from the looseleaf edition have been retained in the CLE edition.

Even experienced parties can be surprised should their expectations not be realized. However, as long as the parties come to see the process as credible, there should be few obstacles that cannot be overcome.

The mediator also needs to establish the behavioral ground rules for the mediation. The mediator may wish to seek input from the parties, especially if they are relatively experienced in the process. In fact, permitting mutual discussion of the governing ground rules can in itself be a crucial first step towards promoting cooperation and problem-solving.

The ground rules should include:

- Order of discussion;

- Prohibitions on interruptions by the other party during the relation of positions;

- Rules regarding breaks during the session; and

- Rules regarding food, beverage and smoking during the session.

In addition, any other issues regarding the basic behavior of the participants that the mediator believes should be clarified at the outset of the process should be set out or discussed. The parties should be given the opportunity to voice any concerns about the basic ground rules to insure their comfort in the process. For example, should a party question the reason for any rule, the mediator will need to provide a logical and rational explanation.

If a party violates a rule, a reference to the underlying rationale for the rule may prove helpful. For example, if a party continually interrupts the other during the initial relation of facts, the mediator should refer the party back to the fundamental concept underlying the "no interruption" ground rule: "Treat others as you wish to be treated."

The ground rules also include the physical and temporal logistics of the process. Logistical factors to be discussed might include:

A Lawyer's Guide to Effective Negotiation and Mediation, CLE edition, is the abridged version of the looseleaf edition designed for use in CLE programs. The section and form numbering from the looseleaf edition have been retained in the CLE edition.

119

- Location of further sessions, both separate and joint;
- How a party or the mediator can request a separate meeting or caucus with the mediator;
- Estimated length of meetings;
- The procedures and timing for handling witnesses;
- Procedures to call a recess or suspension of the session; and
- Rules on the taking and preservation of process notes by the parties and the mediator.

§ 9.9 Stage One—Gathering and Analyzing the Facts

Following the mediator's opening statement and discussion, the focus of the interaction is shifted by the mediator to the dispute. Before issues can be resolved, all relevant information and facts in the dispute need to be made available to the parties and set out for consideration by all parties.

In complex mediations, this information gathering process can occur in a separate caucus with each party before the bargaining process begins. Preferably, a written statement of facts is prepared by each party prior to the mediation for submission to the mediator. This statement includes information both from the parties and from non-party sources.

In relatively simple disputes, the task can be accomplished in an initial joint meeting of the parties. The information gathering process often continues through the mediation if it becomes clear that pieces of information were omitted or misinterpreted.

In the best of situations, the mediator can review a prepared statement of "agreed facts" created by the parties and a list of issues in dispute. Then, additional facts are offered by each party in the presence of the other which maintains the openness of the proceedings at this early stage.

A Lawyer's Guide to Effective Negotiation and Mediation, CLE edition, is the abridged version of the looseleaf edition designed for use in CLE programs. The section and form numbering from the looseleaf edition have been retained in the CLE edition.

There are three procedures for gathering information: interviewing, secondary sources, and observation. Christopher W. Moore, *The Mediation Process: Practical Strategies for Resolving Conflict* (Jossey–Bass Publishers, 1986) at 80. Interviewing, the most commonly used method, helps to build credibility and rapport by creating a direct mediator-party interaction.

Secondary sources are anything that allows the mediator to gather information about the dispute or its background, including business records, minutes of meetings, journal articles and court documents. *Id.*, at 80. In direct observation, the mediator observes the parties, but without intervention. *Id.*, at 80.

The latter two tactics do not involve the parties, nor do they help to build credibility or rapport. They do, however, potentially provide the mediator with more information than the parties might personally be able to remember or relate.

In designing the presentational format of information, the mediator should consider:

- Who speaks first in joint sessions;
- How to prevent the other party from becoming bored or "burned out" during the other party's time;
- What time constraints will be placed on the speakers;
- How emotional expression will be allowed; and
- How interruptions or other disruptive behavior will be handled.

Id., at 89.

Since people relate information in accordance with their own bias and perceptions, accurate information gathering is a difficult task for a mediator. Topics or subject matter that could create distance or trigger embarrassment between a party and the mediator should be avoided at this early stage of the mediation. Sensitive information will have to be explored at some point in the process, but

Notes

the parties should be provided time to get comfortable in the setting, and with the mediator and the process.

In addition to open-ended (narrative seeking) and close-ended (limited response clarifying) questions used to gather information in the initial stages of the mediation, there are other questioning techniques especially useful in mediation:

Question Type:	Usage:
Elaboration	A request for more information regarding a statement
Clarification	A request to clarify a seemingly vague or ambiguous statement
Summary	A question that summarizes the statements and requests confirmation
Repetition	An exact restatement of the previous question to get a more clear or concrete response, or to make an accurate confirmation
Active Listening	A brief restatement which responds to the emotional components of a statement
Confrontation	A question that points out discrepancies or contradictions which arise in the respondent's statements

Id., at 91–92.

In each of the above questions, and especially in a confrontation question, the mediator needs to exert caution and care to insure not offending a party or creating defensiveness. A breakdown in positive tone can lead to a break in the process or jeopardize the credibility of the mediator.

The mediator needs to evaluate the information related by parties and witnesses for its consistency, coherence and completeness. This is part of the storytelling model as it applies in the relating of positions in mediation.

A Lawyer's Guide to Effective Negotiation and Mediation, CLE edition, is the abridged version of the looseleaf edition designed for use in CLE programs. The section and form numbering from the looseleaf edition have been retained in the CLE edition.

If an inconsistency or gap emerges, the mediator should review the notes of the interview, re-read secondary sources and conduct follow-up questioning. *Id.*, at 100. If the inconsistency is not resolved, the mediator should make the conflict explicit and request the party or parties to clarify the information. The process should always be handled by the mediator in a positive manner, without an accusatory or confrontational tone. *Id.*, at 100. The mediator's conduct should always be conducted with the intent of preserving a working atmosphere so that the conflict can be addressed once the general information is set out by all participants.

§ 9.10   Stage Two—Identifying Conflict

After all underlying information has been collected and verified, the mediator needs to identify the points of conflict by categorizing them into one of two categories: unrealistic or genuine. Unrealistic conflicts are those resulting from misperceptions, strong subjective emotions, miscommunication or negative behavior patterns. The mediator should work with the parties to dispose of these conflicts so that genuine conflicts, *i.e.*, points of actual dispute, can be addressed. Once conflict is determined to be genuine, the type or nature of the conflict can be identified.

There are five general types of conflict: interest, structural, factual, value and relational. Christopher W. Moore, *The Mediation Process: Practical Strategies for Resolving Conflict* (Jossey–Bass Publishers, 1986) at 19. Each conflict type consists of its own problem areas and accompanying remedies.

Interest conflicts exist where the parties have mutually exclusive goals: "Party A wants 'X,' and Party B wants 'Y'." The X and Y represent whatever interests are in dispute, i.e., substantive, monetary, procedural, intangible, psychological or social. The mutual exclusivity factor means that if A does get X, B cannot have Y, or vice-versa. The exclusivity may be real or perceived by the parties; regardless, the parties will almost always perceive the conflict to be real, which means the problem is real.

A Lawyer's Guide to Effective Negotiation and Mediation, CLE edition, is the abridged version of the looseleaf edition designed for use in CLE programs. The section and form numbering from the looseleaf edition have been retained in the CLE edition.

§ 9.10

Notes

Structural conflict refers to the dynamics that affect the interactive environment for the parties. These constraints can be imposed on the parties either by internal or external factors. Internal factors include destructive patterns of prior conduct between the parties, unequal allocation of resources, control over or ownership of resources. External factors include physical, environmental, geographic, or time constraints.

Factual conflicts refer to the differences in the information available to the parties. The differences can arise from the method of data collection employed or the interpretation of the data created after collection. Of course, either or both parties can have incorrect information, or may lack a crucial piece of information. Even if all relevant information is available to the parties, they may nevertheless interpret the information differently. Differences over relevance or priority, or variance in the analytical procedures used to interpret the data can ignite conflict.

Value conflicts are based in emotion or morality. They can be grounded in cultural, religious, or ideological differences. Such differences, exhibited in stereotypes and misconceptions, often lead people to evaluate personal behavior or ideas in very different ways. However, even parties who share the same cultural and social spheres can have divergent views which create mutually exclusive goals of the parties.

Relationship conflicts emerge from the personal interaction of the parties. Strongly negative emotions such as hatred or distrust lead to behavior patterns which become the explicit basis for conflict. The absence of communication, the inability of a party to articulate thoughts, and personality differences can all trigger conflict in a relationship. Once the type of genuine conflict is identified, the mediator can focus the interaction on the issues which form the basis of the conflict.

§ 9.11 Stage Three—Identifying Issues

The mediator needs to uncover the specific issues about which the conflict is based. An issue for mediation is any element of a dispute between the parties that can be expressed as one party's interest and that is capable of being effectively addressed by the process. Most major issues are composed of a series of smaller issues, the dissection of which is important to achieve levels of progress towards total agreement.

Moreover, unidentified issues can become stumbling blocks or hidden traps later in the process; much relational work may have to be repeated to maintain progress. In complex cases, there may be so many issues the mediator may wish to create a worksheet to track the issues and their specifics as the process continues. Jay Folberg and Allison Taylor, *Mediation: A Comprehensive Guide to Resolving Conflicts Without Litigation* (Jossey–Bass Publishers, 1985) at 48. In simple disputes, this process is less likely to be necessary.

There is a four stage process that mediators can use to identify the issues to be discussed. Sally Engle Silbey and Susan Merry, "Mediator Settlement Strategies," 8 Law and Policy 7 (1986) at 15–18. First, the mediator looks beyond the current disagreement to broaden the dispute to all possible issues. Second, the mediator selects issues from this range. Third, the mediator restates the issues into negotiable terms. Finally, the mediator may choose or suggest that the parties postpone issues that cannot be resolved at an initial session.

The issues of conflict are not usually circumscribed by the limited area of dispute that has brought the parties into the mediation. The issues should be broadened to include the totality of surrounding circumstances. For example, open-ended inquiries can reveal the prior relationship between the parties, their shared values and experiences.

The issues uncovered through broadening which are important and have a high potential for resolution should first be identified by the mediator or through discussion led by the mediators but with the parties input. William Simkin and Nicholas Friandis, *Mediation and the Dynamics of Collective Bargaining* (BNA, 1986) at 80–81. The importance of the issues and likelihood of their set-

A Lawyer's Guide to Effective Negotiation and Mediation, CLE edition, is the abridged version of the looseleaf edition designed for use in CLE programs. The section and form numbering from the looseleaf edition have been retained in the CLE edition.

125

tlement should be considered to determine where mediation efforts might best be focused.

Issues deemed to be important and relatively easy to settle should top the mediation agenda. Issues deemed to be unimportant or potentially difficult to settle should be addressed early, only if the other factor rates high. An unimportant and difficult issue is best left for resolution later in the process, once the parties have experienced the rewards of compromise and cooperation.

Once issues are selected for the agenda, the mediator should attempt to transform each one into a specific request for action or general behavior. The mediator can also quantify the issue by translating it into a dollar amount, when appropriate. This process removes the emotional factors of blame or revenge which can impede the focus of the mediation. Sally Engle Silbey and Susan Merry, "Mediator Settlement Strategies," 8 Law and Policy 7 (1986) at 17.

Mediators may see the value in postponing discussion of a particular issue. For example, an issue may begin to block the entire process and promote a stalemate. The mediator can point to the advantage of returning to that issue later in the process, once some other more readily resolvable issues are addressed.

The mediator can suggest a contingent agreement that accounts for any postponed issues, or perhaps the reconsideration of these issues after the parties have had time to weigh the effects of the initial agreement. As the mediation proceeds, these issues may work themselves out in the scope of other matters. Conversely, they may not be resolved, but at least all other major concerns are not sidetracked over one difficult point of contention. This process will work absent hidden interests of one or both parties.

Parties will not often reveal their real interests early on in a mediation. This is not always a deliberate tactic; some parties are honestly unaware of their own genuine interests. Other issues are so closely tied to psychological or social factors that lie deep beneath the surface that the party cannot see them with any clarity. The mediator can seek to expose hidden interests through direct questioning utilized in separate caucus, group discussion, or brainstorming sessions.

Uncovering hidden or subconscious interests can also help identify and resolve some types of problem behaviors exhibited by the parties. When combined with the mediator's focus on party interests, the parties will feel some pressure to reveal true interests, or risk losing credibility by not answering or sidestepping the mediator's questions.

Once hidden interests are uncovered, the mediator can insure they do not impede the process. The mediator should first point out the compatible interests between the parties and seek agreement on them. The mediator should then specify the incompatible interests, obtain the parties' recognition and acceptance of them. This recognition and acceptance process, while not insuring subsequent agreement, provides a foundation for more sincere and effective bargaining.

§ 9.12 State Four—Defining the Agenda Structure

Once the nature of the underlying conflict and accompanying specific issues have been identified, the mediator and the parties need to work together to create a structure or agenda for discussion. There are several agenda structures available.

(1) **Ad hoc.** The parties discuss issues in whatever order the issues naturally occur.

(2) **First Issue Then Ad hoc.** The parties agree on the first issue to be discussed and the discussion proceeds naturally thereafter.

(3) **Simple Agenda.** A basic or general order is set. This is not an advisable approach because the parties can manipulate unimportant items to gain leverage in the discussion of others.

(4) **Building Block or Domino Approach.** The parties link related issues together for discussion, or dis-

A Lawyer's Guide to Effective Negotiation and Mediation, CLE edition, is the abridged version of the looseleaf edition designed for use in CLE programs. The section and form numbering from the looseleaf edition have been retained in the CLE edition.

127

cuss the threshold issues first. The intent is that the minor matters will resolve quickly thereafter.

 (5) **Alternating Choice.** One party chooses an issue to discuss, than the other chooses. This structure rarely works for long before disputes arise. For example, the parties may even argue over who will select the first issue to be discussed.

 (6) **Most Important Issue First.** The issues are discussed in an agreed-upon or established order of importance, starting with the most important. The intent is that critical issues will be more quickly resolved.

(7) **Least Difficult Issue First.** The issues are discussed in their perceived order of estimated resolution difficulty, starting with the least difficult. This approach permits the parties to build an effective bargaining relationship prior to tackling the tough issues. In many cases, the easier issues are less important and often traded off in the agreements on other matters.

(8) **Chronological Order.** The parties discuss the issues in the order they arose in the dispute.

Once an agenda has been created, the mediator can formulate a detailed plan of progress. The type and detail of mediation plan varies with the preferences of the mediator. Some mediators prefer highly detailed plans which set out all contingencies; other mediators prefer less detail and more spontaneity in the process. Mediators are encouraged to grant the parties input into the creation of the plan, providing them with a greater sense of commitment. Christopher W. Moore, *The Mediation Process: Practical Strategies for Resolving Conflict* (Jossey–Bass Publishers, 1986) at 104.

When designing the plan the mediator should:

- Identify strategies that will move the parties towards agreement;

- Identify areas or issues of potential deadlock;

- Identify possible contingent responses to specific positions;

- Predict potential problem behavior; and

- Identify actual or perceived power imbalances that can impede the progress of the discussions.

§ 9.13 Stage Five—Search for Remedies and Generating Options

The search for resolution commences with a series of tactics associated with specific conflict and issues and should therefore be considered in light of the identified conflict type. Christopher W. Moore, *The Mediation Process: Practical Strategies for Resolving Conflict* (Jossey–Bass Publishers, 1986) at 27.

The remedies for interest conflicts include:

- Shifting the focus of the interaction from party positions to their interests and developing solutions which address these interests;

- Searching for ways to expand options so neither party fails to meet their needs;

- Prioritizing interests and developing trade-offs; and

- Searching for objective criteria against which resolutions can be sought.

Remedies to structural conflicts include:

- Defining and changing the disputants' roles in the process to provide flexibility;

- Modifying destructive patterns of behavior;

- Reallocating control or ownership of resources;

- Establishing a fair and mutually acceptable decision-making process;

- Moving the parties from positional bargaining to interest-based bargaining;

- Changing time and deadline structure; and

- Changing meeting location.

Notes

Remedies for factual conflicts include:

- Searching out additional relevant information;
- Separating the parties for clarification of facts by the mediator;
- Agreeing on information gathering procedures;
- Developing common criteria to evaluate the information gathered; and
- Using neutral experts for outside opinions.

Remedies for value conflicts include:

- Moving the focus from positions to interests;
- Assisting the parties to realize the differences in their viewpoints;
- Searching for object criteria against which a solution can be formulated;
- Creating solutions which address the values of all parties;
- Constructive venting of emotions; and
- Prioritizing interests and uncovering possible trade-offs.

Remedies for relationship conflicts include:

- Allowing emotions to be vented under controlled conditions;
- Correcting misperceptions, breaking down stereotypes, and enhancing positive perceptions;
- Improving communication by soliciting an exchange of opinions and suggestions;
- Blocking negative behavior patterns through structural changes; and
- Encouraging positive attitudes in the resolution-seeking process.

Once the actions to effectuate the remedies are selected, the mediator needs to implement the remedy by intervening to take the effectuating actions. Implementation may include trial and error until the mediator's work takes effect.

If resolution of the conflict results, then the action taken was proper; if the conflict persists, the action can

A Lawyer's Guide to Effective Negotiation and Mediation, CLE edition, is the abridged version of the looseleaf edition designed for use in CLE programs. The section and form numbering from the looseleaf edition have been retained in the CLE edition.

be revised or a new one selected. If subsequent actions fail, then the conflict may have been misdiagnosed necessitating an additional gathering of information and repetition of the process.

While mediators work to resolve the inherent conflicts between the parties, they also initiate a search to generate options for settlement with regard for party interests. The process of creating options is the most creative part of the mediation. The mediator is a resource person for the parties; the importance of an extensive knowledge of the subject matter of the dispute becomes apparent at this stage. Jay Folberg and Allison Taylor, *Mediation: A Comprehensive Guide to Resolving Conflicts Without Litigation* (Jossey–Bass Publishers, 1985) at 53. However, the mediator needs to be cautious of how she uses her substantive knowledge; she must always preserve the image of impartiality.

The process of creating options consists of two central tasks:

(1) assisting the parties to articulate known options; and

(2) developing new options.

Creating options is done through a variety of interactive tools:

- Brainstorming (See § 2.21, *supra*);
- Discussion groups or subgroups;
- Discussion of hypothetical and plausible scenarios; and
- Using outside sources.

Christopher W. Moore, *The Mediation Process: Practical Strategies for Resolving Conflict* (Jossey–Bass Publishers, 1986) at 212–216.

In many cases, parties become attached to their positions and are not willing to consider alternatives. The mediator's task at this stage is to get the parties to shift away from their positions and recognize the importance of compromise and making joint efforts to meet underlying interests of all parties. In this way, the mediator serves as the parties' "agent of reality" getting the parties to critically evaluate their expressed positions.

Unrealistic goals or demands of a party need to be pointed out. By creating doubt in an unrealistic position, the mediator can lead parties to both consider broader underlying interests and to refocus their actions accordingly. Jay Folberg and Allison Taylor, *Mediation: A Comprehensive Guide to Resolving Conflicts Without Litigation* (Jossey–Bass Publishers, 1985) at 55. The mediator needs a commitment from the parties to, at a minimum, explore the various options. Not until a party's commitment to a position has been lowered or tempered can the mediator focus the discussion on generating mutually acceptable options for settlement.

§ 9.14 Stage Six—Assessing Options

Eventually the parties generate enough viable options from which to create a mutually agreeable settlement. The mediator's role in this part of the process is to assist the parties in that effort. Any remedy accepted by the parties will need to be appropriate to the nature of the conflict.

Assessment of options should include:

- The needs and interests of the parties and anyone else who will be affected by the agreement;
- Relevant predictions of future behavioral, economic, and social changes and direction; and
- Legal and financial norms which will guide the solution structure.

Jay Folberg and Allison Taylor, *Mediation: A Comprehensive Guide to Resolving Conflicts Without Litigation* (Jossey–Bass Publishers, 1985) at 50.

The mediator re-examines the information and interests of the parties in light of these factors and options are assessed with regard to party interests, vis-a-vis their costs and benefits. Mediator preferences play no role in the agreement; the mediator considers only what terms the parties can live with in the future.

In the event the assessment process creates a stalemate, the mediator can suggest that the parties conduct a trial period for one reasonable option. The trial period allows the parties to directly experience the consequences of a particular option or option package. This is an extremely useful approach when both parties like an option, but one believes unequivocally that it will not work while the other is equally convinced that it will meet the interests of all parties. *Id.*, at 52.

§ 9.15 Stage Seven—Reaching Resolution

The selection of an option can produce anxiety for parties; selection requires a commitment to a course of action. The mediator may need to encourage the parties to take the seemingly risky step of making a decision. The mediator can assist the parties to select an option by suggesting some supportive approaches:

- The "Half-a-Loaf" approach: the parties agree to compromise because "half a loaf is better than none;"

- "Expanding the Pie": the parties search for new or unknown resources to uncover a win-win solution; or

- "Horsetrading": the parties exchange or link options as necessary to create a workable package.

The mediator can also create other options for the parties, but needs to maintain the appearance of impartiality and must explain any perceived bias.

*

A Lawyer's Guide to Effective Negotiation and Mediation, CLE edition, is the abridged version of the looseleaf edition designed for use in CLE programs. The section and form numbering from the looseleaf edition have been retained in the CLE edition.

Chapter 10

MEDIATION TECHNIQUES

Table of Sections

WESTLAW Electronic Research
See WESTLAW Electronic Research Guide preceding the Summary of Contents.

Notes

§ 10.1 Mediator Roles—From Passive to Active

The role or persona assumed by a mediator will be dictated by the needs of the parties and the nature of the dispute. In general, the mediator's role varies along a spectrum ranging from passive/indirect to active/direct. The former type describes a mediator who simply arranges meetings, leads neutral discussions, or maintains an orderly debate. Howard Raiffa, "Mediation of Conflicts," 12 Amer.Behav.Sci. 195 (Dec. 1983) at p. 196. A more direct but passive mediator might propose settlements that the parties are reluctant to tender themselves for fear of showing weakness to the other party. Lawrence Susskind and Connie Ozawa, "Mediated Negotiation in the Public Sector," 12 Amer.Behav.Sci. 255 (Dec. 1983) at 256.

Active mediators are often thought of as "dealmakers", "muscle mediators" and "neutral third negotiators;" the passive mediator is often seen as an "orchestrator" or "scrivener." In essence, the quality being differentiated revolves around the relative active or passive nature of the mediators. An active/directive mediator, for example, will overtly control the proceedings and guide the development of a settlement.

Whatever role the mediator adopts needs to be employed so as to gain the trust of the parties. Trust and

---

A Lawyer's Guide to Effective Negotiation and Mediation, CLE edition, is the abridged version of the looseleaf edition designed for use in CLE programs. The section and form numbering from the looseleaf edition have been retained in the CLE edition.

Lisnek Effective Negotiation & Mediation—6
CLE Edition

135

integrity are critical in mediation, "Just as nature abhors a vacuum, the negotiation process abhors the absence of trust." Thomas Colosi, "Negotiation in the Public and Private Sectors: A Core Model," 12 Amer.Behav.Sci. 229, (Dec. 1983) at 238. A mediator wins the trust of the parties by demonstrating impartiality; this integrity plays an especially important role when the interaction between the parties reaches a deadlock. In such a case, the requisite cooperative atmosphere is in serious jeopardy or no longer exists.

Mediators should stress the importance of cooperation throughout the process. A positive atmosphere relies on each side's having an opportunity to present their views in an open and constructive manner. Parties, while willing to assist the mediator in fact-finding, will resist any overt or perceived attempt by a mediator to control them or their conduct. A skillful mediator can use the fact-finding process to maintain interactions while guiding the discussion through its moments of conflict.

Active mediators use more manipulative techniques than do passive mediators, each style representing a pattern of mediator attitude and conduct. The shift in mediator technique from passive to active can be viewed along a spectrum.

Passive
↑

- Urging of the parties to agree to talk
- Helping of the parties to understand the mediation process
- Carrying of messages between the parties
- Setting of an agenda for the process
- Providing for a good environment for negotiations
- Maintaining of order
- Helping of the parties to understand the issues
- Revealing of unrealistic goals
- Helping to create options
- Active helping of the parties to negotiate

↓
Active
- Persuading of the parties to accept a particular option

Leonard Riskin and James Westbrook, *Dispute Resolution and Lawyers* (West Publishing, 1987) at 92.

Naturally, few mediators' styles can be labeled as being solely active or passive. The distinction simply represents opposite ends of a spectrum along which mediator behaviors fall. Some situations or types of conflict may necessitate the use of a particular approach. In fact, many mediators are chosen for specific cases because of their style. Sally Engle Silbey and Susan Merry, "Mediator Settlement Strategies," 8 Law and Policy 7 (1986) at p. 19.

Most mediators use a variety of techniques as needed during the mediation session, and which are in accord with their personal style. D. Kolb, *The Mediators* (MIT Press, 1983) at 40–41. A mediator's style tends to become more grounded and standard as experience level increases. Sally Engle Silbey and Susan Merry, "Mediator Settlement Strategies," 8 Law and Policy 7 (1986) at 19. The grounding reflects the reactions of the mediator as she sees what works and what doesn't. Certainly, reactions will vary with the situation and personality of the parties. In general, the mediator will build a general sense of what types of techniques work in particular situations.

Mediator style is often reflected in the emphasis placed by the mediator in the session on the quality of the parties' relationship. Mediation that actively stresses emotions and communication is labelled "therapeutic." *Id.*, at 19–22. Mediation focused on party interests, such as economic concerns, is called "bargaining" and is a traditional style of mediation.

This difference is important in arenas of mediation that involve extensive personal contact and therapeutically-oriented tactics, such as community or divorce dispute resolution. In most other mediation arenas, the therapeutic component of the parties' relationship is of less import.

An active mediator is very involved in the process and substance of the mediation. The active mediator believes that the parties are unlikely to reach an agreement without considerable participation by the mediator. D.

Kolb, *The Mediators* (MIT Press, 1983) at 33. Communications between the parties are rigidly controlled by the mediator who may also seek to alter the discussion as necessary to promote agreement. The mediator can become an advocate for each party's position as it is presented in the mediation.

The role adopted by mediator Henry Kissinger during the Middle East negotiations of the 1970's, for example, illustrates an active/directive approach as a mediator:

(1) Exclusively controlled all communications between the parties;

(2) Actively persuaded the parties to make concessions;

(3) Acted as a scapegoat to deflect the parties' anger and frustrations from each other;

(4) Masked the bargaining power of the parties;

(5) Proposed possible settlements; and

(6) Created and maintained the talks.

Lawrence Susskind and Connie Ozawa, "Mediated Negotiation in the Public Sector," 12 Amer.Behav.Sci. 255 (Dec. 1983) at 272–273.

Passive mediators take a more relaxed approach to the mediation process believing that the parties can create an acceptable settlement with minimum interference from the mediator. Passive mediators exhibit little interest in the substance of what is being discussed. The parties address each other directly, with the mediator often fading into the background. D. Kolb, *The Mediators* (MIT Press, 1983) at 59.

When the parties caucus privately with the mediator, the communication that is channelled through the mediator is routinely recorded and re-read verbatim. Regardless of style, mediation requires a meshing of party positions.

The mediator needs to assist the parties to behave or think differently, and in such a way that they are unaware of the source of the new thought or action. Sally Engle Silbey and Susan Merry, "Mediator Settlement Strat-

---

egies," 8 Law and Policy 7 (1986) at n. 5. If the parties were able to reach an agreement by themselves, they would not have required the services of a mediator. Thus, it is the task of the mediator to get the parties out of their entrenched positions and into settlement.

The mediator accomplishes this shift by monitoring the communications between the parties, focusing the discussion towards settlement and narrowing the issues away from those for which agreement is impossible. *Id.*, at 5–16. Mediator expertise and skills are exercised to select tactics appropriate to the situation. These skills combined with the inherent prestige of the role of the mediator, the ability to work with the knowledge of the parties, and the case issues, all highlight the legitimate nature of the mediator's effort.

§ 10.2 Mediation Tactics—In General

Mediation tactics can be categorized into three basic types: communication tactics, substantive tactics, and procedural tactics. Many tactics do not fall neatly into one category or another, but involve a combination of the categories. William Simkin and Nicholas Friandis, *Mediation and the Dynamics of Collective Bargaining* (BNA, 1986) at 59. Once reviewing the arsenal of available tactics, the mediator needs to make careful selection to insure the appropriate means are used at each point in the mediation.

§ 10.3 Mediation Tactics—Communication Based

Communication tactics enhance the connection between the parties by controlling the lines or content of the communication. Thus, communication tactics are powerful when the parties are separated for private caucus. By choosing what to communicate, and how to do it, the mediator can gain extensive control over substantive issues during caucus with a party. Sally Engle Silbey and Susan Merry, "Mediator Settlement Strategies," 8 Law and Policy 7 (1986) at 14–15. Communication tactics are used to further the mediator's goal of improving the direct communication between the parties.

A Lawyer's Guide to Effective Negotiation and Mediation, CLE edition, is the abridged version of the looseleaf edition designed for use in CLE programs. The section and form numbering from the looseleaf edition have been retained in the CLE edition.

Notes

(1) **Direct Communication.** A mediator may intentionally relinquish control of the lines of communication to require direct communication between the parties. The acceptance or rejection of this tactic by the parties is immediate and direct. This will be a tactic of the passive mediator who prefers direct party contact requiring the parties to bargain with a minimum of interference. Active mediators, because they prefer more control over the interaction, will prefer separate meetings. D. Kolb, *The Mediators* (MIT Press, 1983) at 59–61.

Direct communication allows the parties to vent emotions constructively, have them addressed, and hopefully resolved. In many cases, a party needs to vent emotion directly; channelling the feelings through the mediator does not have the same resolving effect. Conversely, the mediator can try to suppress a party's emotion if such expression would only be destructive to the process. Christopher W. Moore, *The Mediation Process: Practical Strategies for Resolving Conflict* (Jossey–Bass Publishers, 1986) at 131–132.

(2) **Mediator as Conduit.** The mediator as a "conduit" of information repeats, verbatim and with permission, statements or proposals made by a party during caucus. D. Kolb, *The Mediators* (MIT Press, 1983) at 96–98. The mediator makes it clear to the parties that the message has not been modified in any way. The report is delivered in an emotionally neutral manner leaving the emotional state of the parties to be inferred from the message itself. This tactic is often used by passive mediators who promote interaction between the parties by actions or words of the parties.

(3) **Mediator as Surrogate.** The mediator as "surrogate" communicator repeats a communication verbatim, but adds to it the perceived underlying reasons or justifications for the proposal. In short, the mediator acts as a surrogate of the other party, but without becoming an advocate. Missing information or descriptions of emotional states can also be conveyed by the mediator. The mediator uses this technique to shape the responding parties' arguments and responses without substantive inter-

ference, making it a valuable tool for both active and passive mediators. *Id.*, at 96–98, 108.

(4) **Reshaping.** By changing or embellishing a statement or proposal between the parties, a mediator can reshape communication so as to improve its effectiveness. Unlike surrogate communication, mediators who use reshaping do not separate a party's statement from their own. Reshaping can remove or add emotionally charged language, supply missing information, or set out or explain underlying rationale. The technique is used quite a bit by active mediators, but passive mediators will avoid this tactic due to its highly manipulative appearance. *Id.*, at 108.

(5) **Clarification.** When a party has a question for the other side, or does not understand something related in the mediation, the mediator can ask the other side for a clarification. This tactic gives the mediator some degree of control over both the question and the answer and is useful for preventing misconceptions between the parties. The technique is useful in providing the answering party with insight into the other side's understanding of the issues and priorities. Passive mediators prefer this tactic to reshaping because it is less intrusive to the mediation process.

Communication tactics generally involve little mediator intrusion into the substance of the process. The main concern in using these tactics is the unintended hindrance of communication. Mediators who give their own opinion or clarification as to the rationale or position of a party create a risk of fostering miscommunication. Misinterpretation can cause delays in the process by shifting the mediation in a less positive direction, such as leading a party to change its position in an unnecessary or obstructive manner.

§ 10.4 Mediation Tactics—Procedural Based

Procedural tactics affect the process of mediation itself. These tactics can be utilized early on in the process to create an initial mediation plan, or during the mediation should a change of plan become necessary. Proce-

A Lawyer's Guide to Effective Negotiation and Mediation, CLE edition, is the abridged version of the looseleaf edition designed for use in CLE programs. The section and form numbering from the looseleaf edition have been retained in the CLE edition.

141

dural tactics can be exercised in a concealed and unobtrusive manner.

(1) **Caucus.** Arranging separate meetings, or "caucuses," with each party is a technique almost universally employed by mediators. Caucusing can serve many positive functions in mediation and it makes possible the use of many other tactics. Caucusing permits ideas and proposals to be discussed, considered, altered, or adopted in a confidential setting. Parties do not have to worry about appearing weak or losing face by stepping outside the joint session. The benefit is the mediator's ability to conduct the mediation in an open and frank atmosphere.

Caucusing can also be useful to allow the parties in highly emotionally charged disputes to vent their feelings. It is true that the venting may occur in a way that is less satisfying than head-to-head confrontation and when emotions are so strong that they would severely or permanently disrupt the process.

The mediator provides diplomacy by keeping the parties separate by controlling the lines of communication. In these situations, it is important to control the passage of the parties from the waiting room to the mediation room and to prevent any encounter between the parties until emotions settle. W. Richard Evarts, *Winning Through Accommodation: The Mediator's Handbook* (Kendall–Hunt, 1983) at 75.

When utilizing a caucus, the mediator should always speak to *each* party, even if there is only a need to speak to one; this avoids any appearance of taking sides or impropriety. This does not mean that the duration of each caucus need be of equal length. The mediator should begin each caucus with personal rapport-building discussion to give the parties the feeling that they can speak freely in an environment that is focused on them alone.

The mediator should also be certain to inform each party at the beginning of the caucus session that everything discussed in the caucus will be confidential; this promise furthers an atmosphere of free exchange. Needless to say, the mediator must keep this promise, or risk a

A Lawyer's Guide to Effective Negotiation and Mediation, CLE edition, is the abridged version of the looseleaf edition designed for use in CLE programs. The section and form numbering from the looseleaf edition have been retained in the CLE edition.

142

certain loss of credibility in the eyes of the offended party, and perhaps all parties.

The mediator may ask a party during the caucus to clarify whether specified information may be revealed in the joint session, either by the mediator or the party. Permission to disclose concessions made in caucus must also be obtained before anything may be said in joint session.

The timing of beginning the caucus can be critical. Usually, a caucus is best held after a productive joint session, but before the remaining entrenched positions lead to distrust or hostility. The specific timing cannot be detailed for every situation; the mediator needs to analyze each situation and determine when a caucus would serve the process.

Caucus can be useful at other times in the mediation, such as just prior to the final bargaining of the agreement when specific formulas and procedures for an agreement are defined. Christopher W. Moore, "The Caucus: Private Meetings that Promote Settlement," 16 Med.Q. 87 (1987) at 90–91.

(2) **Recess.** The mediator can propose to postpone further meetings or the mediation itself if the atmosphere becomes harsh or angry. Postponement can prevent a single difficult moment or statement from undoing weeks of work and progress; it permits the situation to cool. William Simkin and Nicholas Friandis, *Mediation and the Dynamics of Collective Bargaining* (BNA, 1986) at 60. Recess also permits consideration of a new idea that has been introduced by a party or the mediator.

Permitting the parties time to seriously consider alternatives can be an effective stalemate breaker. A short recess can be useful near the end of a long mediation session to give the parties and the mediator a chance to rest; the resultant energy produced by a short rest can often produce a successful closing.

A short recess can also be used as a "mediator's caucus" permitting the mediator some time to think about the next move. R. Castrey and C. Castrey, "Timing: A

A Lawyer's Guide to Effective Negotiation and Mediation, CLE edition, is the abridged version of the looseleaf edition designed for use in CLE programs. The section and form numbering from the looseleaf edition have been retained in the CLE edition.

Mediator's Best Friend," 16 Med.Q. 15 (1987) at 15–16. This can be an effective tactic during particularly heated or fast-moving mediations. It can also be useful in those situations where there is more than one mediator because it allows them to share and coordinate their thoughts and plans in confidence.

(3) **Keeping the Feet to the Fire.** The closing stage of a mediation may require the parties to negotiate continuously without rest. This technique may be used in times of impending deadline, such as a strike date, that would otherwise end the mediation process. In other situations, the parties may be "on a roll" and the mediator senses that rest will break the momentum; a party who leaves the bargaining table may quickly discover new reasons for disagreement.

Continuing the mediation may also lead a party to abandon a hardened position and agree to compromise. The mediator should monitor to guard against compromise from physical exhaustion. The ultimate feelings can be regret and a desire to rescind. All parties need to be physically able to handle the stress of a continuing session or a break should be given in the process.

(4) **Changing Location.** A mediator may wish to change the location of the mediation. Where one party may be disadvantaged by the current location because it is more familiar to one side or the other, perhaps providing that party with easier access to information, the mediator should consider moving the mediation to a more neutral site. A mediation might also be moved if the parties become distracted by some internal or outside influence. Moving the parties to a more isolated or private location can help reduce these distractions.

(5) **Using Deadlines.** Deadlines present pressure to settle. If a deadline is set in a mediation, the mediator can remind the parties of the consequences of missing the deadline. External deadlines may also have been established by the parties, or there may be external deadlines that are beyond the control of the parties, such as strike dates or Congressional funding deadlines. If no deadline

A Lawyer's Guide to Effective Negotiation and Mediation, CLE edition, is the abridged version of the looseleaf edition designed for use in CLE programs. The section and form numbering from the looseleaf edition have been retained in the CLE edition.

144

is established, active mediators may create and set one, but will need to state valid reasons for it, if the move is questioned by the parties. *Id.*, at 17.

One type of mediator-established deadline is a natural, internal deadline. An internal deadline emerges in a long mediation session when the parties are tired but still desire to settle. For example, the mediator can state that midnight or some other designated time will be the point beyond which no further work can effectively be conducted.

(6) **Strategic Suggestions.** In addition to suggestions on settlement proposals or party positions, the mediator can make recommendations to the parties about how they should approach the mediation process as a whole. The mediator can use this tactic to lead the parties into a mindset that will naturally oblige settlement.

A strategic suggestion is greatly appreciated by an inexperienced party who becomes frozen in indecision out of fear of making the wrong move. This tactic is very popular with passive mediators because the proper suggestion can allow the mediator to virtually withdraw from the rest of the mediation. D. Kolb, *The Mediators* (MIT Press, 1983) at 108.

(7) **Threats.** Threats can take many forms: mediators can threaten to withdraw, they can begin pointing to less palpable alternatives like arbitration or litigation, or they can threaten that even the mediation process will become drawn out. *Id.*, at 98. It should be used rarely and with great caution.

Threats can be real or intended as a bluff, but the mediator should be prepared to carry them through. Failure, or an inability to carry through on a threat, will not only bar the use of the tactic by that mediator in the future, it will also jeopardize the mediator's credibility with those parties.

As a tactic, a threat is highly manipulative. It is based in coercion. Not surprisingly, passive mediators never use threat as a tactic. In fact, even most active mediators avoid using threats as they can lead the parties to

---

A Lawyer's Guide to Effective Negotiation and Mediation, CLE edition, is the abridged version of the looseleaf edition designed for use in CLE programs. The section and form numbering from the looseleaf edition have been retained in the CLE edition.

145

become defensive or angry. Even if a threat works, it can produce unexpected results; people backed into a corner are unpredictable. In most cases, the mediator hopes simply that the shock value of the threat itself will trigger the parties to act in a positive manner.

While procedural tactics typically go unnoticed by the parties, those experienced in mediation will detect procedural change. As such, procedural tactics should be exercised carefully. Similarly, if the change affects a part of the plan that has been revealed to the parties, they will become curious about the alteration.

While the authority of mediators permits them to alter the mediation plan without challenge by the parties, mediators are best advised to reveal the motive behind any procedural change; failure to do so could diminish the parties' trust in that mediator and render long term damage to the reputation of that mediator.

§ 10.5 Mediation Tactics—Substantive Based

While communication and procedural tactics affect the substantive content of the bargaining, the mediator can also take direct actions designed to change a party's position or to force a particular action. Most substantive tactics are specific in need, design and timing.

(1) **Activation of Commitments.** If the parties become discouraged or the interaction reaches impasse, the mediator can attempt to regain commitment to the process by reminding the parties of the goals that first brought them into the process. Sally Engle Silbey and Susan Merry, "Mediator Settlement Strategies," 8 Law and Policy 7 (1986) at 18. The mediator can use two sources of values for this tactic: societal norms that promote negotiation, and communicative expectations which illustrate how the parties ought to act. The mediator can also reconfirm the commitments of the parties made or revealed during prior parts of the process.

(2) **Cost Assessment.** Requiring the parties to make a cost assessment of their demands will quantify the issues of the dispute. The parties come to realize through

---

A Lawyer's Guide to Effective Negotiation and Mediation, CLE edition, is the abridged version of the looseleaf edition designed for use in CLE programs. The section and form numbering from the looseleaf edition have been retained in the CLE edition.

146

this objective criteria the direct economic costs and advantages of any specific proposed action. This tactic is valuable when there are multiple or complicated issues to resolve. Not every issue is quantifiable, but those that can be translated into such terms are easier to resolve. Because of its usefulness, both active and passive mediators use this tactic quite commonly.

(3) **Deflating Extreme Positions.** Parties often enter mediation with unrealistic goals or positions. This is certainly the case where mediation is used as the last alternative to litigation or arbitration. In mediation, of course, if the parties don't retreat from their extreme positions, compromise becomes impossible.

There are two ways the mediator can deflate a party's position or goal: (1) by comparing the position to a seemingly objective one; or (2) by expressing the mediator's own opinion, thereby creating a subjective comparison. By pointing out how a position or proposal deviates from accepted societal norms, the mediator causes the party to adopt a more realistic focus. The norm can be based in a substantive area, or in other disputes handled during the mediator's career.

The power of the mediator's own opinion will weigh heavily on the parties depending upon the experience and perceived credibility of the mediator. A sharply focused statement or opinion by the mediator backed with significant experience will strongly influence the parties.

Regardless of the approach used, the tactic of deflation should only be used during separate party caucus. The nature of the tactic requires a challenge to the party or its position, but the mediator will still wish to preserve trust and a good working atmosphere. Failure to exercise the technique privately can produce a party who becomes embarrassed or angered in joint session. William Simkin and Nicholas Friandis, *Mediation and the Dynamics of Collective Bargaining* (BNA, 1986) at 82.

(4) **Mediator Opinion in Joint Session.** By rendering an opinion in joint session, the mediator can try to create movement in the position of a party. The mediator

A Lawyer's Guide to Effective Negotiation and Mediation, CLE edition, is the abridged version of the looseleaf edition designed for use in CLE programs. The section and form numbering from the looseleaf edition have been retained in the CLE edition.

should maintain the appearance of neutrality whenever giving an opinion. In joint session, an opinion tends to be general and not directly linked to a specific action. The mediator allows the parties to make the connection between the opinion and the suggested action. Nearly all mediators use this tactic, with active mediators relying on the technique quite commonly. D. Kolb, *The Mediators* (MIT Press, 1983) at 108.

(5) **Mediator Suggestion.** If a general opinion does not assist the interaction, then the mediator can make a specific suggestion as to a course of action. Suggestions are a more forceful device than are opinions. A suggestion does not require the party to figure out what action is desired; the desired end is made explicit.

The best suggestions are those that reach beyond compromise. Mediators' suggestions should be creative and should make use of their experience and knowledge. Passive mediators customarily avoid making suggestions; active mediators tend to offer fewer suggestions than they do opinions. D. Kolb, *The Mediators* (MIT Press, 1983) at 108.

(6) **Clarification.** If time is of the essence and the mediator fully understands the parties and the issues, the mediator can offer clarifications instead of caucusing with all parties. Although the technique saves time, there is a danger of mistake by the mediator. This version of clarification fails to provide feedback to either side on what the other side is considering. The possibility of mistake is always reduced whenever questions are conveyed between the parties to measure their own understanding.

(7) **"What Do You Think They Will Do?"** In caucus, the mediator can ask each party to speculate as to the other side's position, underlying interests, or possible movements.

This placement of burden requires each side to reach its own understanding of the other party and the basis of opposition. This exercise should move the parties into the realm of realistic solutions. In those cases where a party's

A Lawyer's Guide to Effective Negotiation and Mediation, CLE edition, is the abridged version of the looseleaf edition designed for use in CLE programs. The section and form numbering from the looseleaf edition have been retained in the CLE edition.

statement of its opponent's position and needs is accurate, a solution can sometimes be created swiftly.

Misuse of a substantive tactic can impair the mediator's image of impartiality. Many of these tactics, such as position deflation, create the appearance that the mediator is siding with the other party because they are used during caucus. One party is unable to witness that the other side is pressured in a similar way. If these substantive tactics are used only with one party, the mediator needs to exert extreme care to preserve apparent and actual impartiality.

Substantive tactics can seriously affect the actual content of the agreement. Therefore, the mediator needs to exercise care not to abuse these tactics, such that they overrule the will of the parties. The result in such a case would be a settlement created for the mediator and not the parties.

In substantive areas requiring specific expertise, the mediator can make use of an outside assistant to provide that expertise. Environmental and public interest disputes often involve experienced assistants.

This assistance can help the mediator in many ways. The assistant can help the mediator uncover technical issues, determine their priority and make explicit any hidden rationale. The assistant can also help the mediator determine the realm of potential concessions for each party.

*

A Lawyer's Guide to Effective Negotiation and Mediation, CLE edition, is the abridged version of the looseleaf edition designed for use in CLE programs. The section and form numbering from the looseleaf edition have been retained in the CLE edition.

Chapter 11

THE LAW AND ETHICS OF MEDIATION

Table of Sections

WESTLAW Electronic Research

See WESTLAW Electronic Research Guide preceding the Summary of Contents.

Notes

§ 11.1 Confidentiality—Law

The emphasis in mediation is certainly on the monitoring of interpersonal dynamics between the parties. However, the mediator must also remain concerned with the legal and ethical considerations that govern the process and the validity of the final agreement.

At the head of the legal and ethical considerations is the need to preserve the confidentiality of the disclosures made by any and all parties during the process. For that matter, there is a strong need to preserve all disclosures made in the process as this furthers the underlying purpose to achieve resolution.

The preservation of party confidentiality is essential to the process of mediation. Without confidentiality, the process would be irreparably harmed. The underlying importance of confidentiality:

- Allows the parties freedom to divulge all necessary information for the process to work;

- Frees mediators in their statements, actions, and tactics;

A Lawyer's Guide to Effective Negotiation and Mediation, CLE edition, is the abridged version of the looseleaf edition designed for use in CLE programs. The section and form numbering from the looseleaf edition have been retained in the CLE edition.

151

- Prevents the unfair use of mediation as a substitute for discovery in subsequent litigation;

- Protects the rights of parties who select mediation because of its underlying privacy;

- Prevents the subsequent use of disclosed statements or evidence by mediators who are connected with a regulatory or prosecutorial agency;

- Protects the mediators' image of fairness by not forcing them to take sides or participate in subsequent litigation; and

- Protects mediators from the harassment of subpoenas by the parties in subsequent litigation.

The lawyer who serves as a mediator is governed not only by any existing rules of mediator conduct, but is also responsible for complying with the rules or code of professional responsibility for lawyers as well. Proper conduct is imperative.

Although the importance of confidentiality is easy to establish, its parameters and applications present more difficult issues. An analysis of confidentiality in mediation requires consideration of the following questions:

(1) What does confidentiality cover?

- statements?—by whom?
  - the mediator?
  - the parties?
  - any non-party participants?
  - others?
- evidence revealed during the process?—by whom?
  - the parties?
  - any non-party participants?
- the mediator's notes/opinions/recommendations?
- the fact that a settlement was reached?
- the settlement terms?

A Lawyer's Guide to Effective Negotiation and Mediation, CLE edition, is the abridged version of the looseleaf edition designed for use in CLE programs. The section and form numbering from the looseleaf edition have been retained in the CLE edition.

Under the Federal Rules of Evidence, a careful look at the applicable rule suggests the exercise of caution in evaluating confidentiality.

Federal Rule of Evidence 408 states: (WESTLAW: US–RULES database, **ci(fre   +5   408)**)

> Evidence of (1) furnishing or offering or promising to furnish, or (2) accepting or offering or promising to accept, a valuable consideration in compromising or attempting to compromise a claim which was disputed as to either validity or amount, is not admissible to prove liability for or invalidity of the claim or its amount. Evidence of conduct or statements made in compromise negotiations is likewise not admissible. . . .

This rule prevents the use of evidence obtained or statements made in settlement proceedings from being used in subsequent litigation. Most states have adopted this provision either verbatim, or with little substantive change.

In jurisdictions where FRE 408 has been adopted without the mediation modification, there is some concern over whether such proceedings are covered. Where its application is clear, FRE 408 covers anything said or revealed in mediation, regardless of whether it was disclosed by a party or a non-party participant. Its coverage is also not dependent upon the success of the attempts to settle; even failed mediation sessions are covered. Certainly, there is great value to this extended coverage.

If disclosures from failed sessions were considered admissable, the entire proceedings would be tainted and parties would be guarded; they would not know whether their disclosures were going to be protected until they learn whether an agreement can be created.

The coverage of FRE 408 is far from absolute. In fact, the rule only covers usage of the protected statements or evidence in court; it does not protect against their use in any out of court or other less formal adjudicatory settings, such as administrative or legislative hearings.

A Lawyer's Guide to Effective Negotiation and Mediation, CLE edition, is the abridged version of the looseleaf edition designed for use in CLE programs. The section and form numbering from the looseleaf edition have been retained in the CLE edition.

153

What FRE 408 actually prevents from being used in court is strictly limited as well:

> . . . . This rule does not require the exclusion of any evidence otherwise discoverable merely because it is present in the course of compromise negotiations. This rule also does not require exclusion when the evidence is offered for another purpose, such as proving bias or prejudice of a witness, negativing a contention of undue delay, or proving an effort to obstruct a criminal investigation or prosecution.

As long as the evidence or the statements made in mediation do not go towards the validity of the claim or the amount of liability, it is admissible. The exceptions listed in FRE 408, though fairly wide in range in and of themselves, are not exclusive. Furthermore, if the evidence or statement sought to be protected could have been discovered through some means other than the mediation process, it will likewise be admissible.

Considering the broad scope of modern discovery rules, along with the wide range of the exceptions to this rule, it appears that much of what is said or revealed during mediation can be admitted through an exception; caution is urged when sensitive information may be revealed.

The importance of mediation confidentiality has led many states to enact statutes ensuring confidentiality in mediation; some of these statutes provide direct changes to state evidence rules; other laws are more limited or more specific. 30 states currently have confidentiality provisions. The following states have broadly worded provisions: **Colorado**, C.R.S.A. § 13–22–307 (1991); **Florida**, Fla.Stat. § 44.201 (1990); **Massachusetts**, Mass.Ann.Laws ch. 233, § 23c (1992); **Oklahoma**, 12 Okl.St. § 1805 (1991); and **Texas**, § 154.053(b); other states with limited statutory language include: **Arizona**, A.R.S. § 12–134 (1992); **Arkansas**, Ark.Stat.Ann. § 11-2-204 (1991); **California**, Cal.Civ.Code § 4351.6 (1991), Cal.Evid.Code § 1152.2 (1991); **Connecticut**, Conn.Gen.Stat. § 10–153f (1990); **Illinois**, Ill.Rev.Stat.

A Lawyer's Guide to Effective Negotiation and Mediation, CLE edition, is the abridged version of the looseleaf edition designed for use in CLE programs. The section and form numbering from the looseleaf edition have been retained in the CLE edition.

154

ch. 37, par. 856 (1991); **Indiana**, Burns Ind.Code Ann. § 15-7-6-6 (farming debt), § 22-9-1-6 (Civil Rights) (1991); **Iowa**, Iowa Code § 679.12 (1989); **Kansas**, K.S.A. § 23-605 (1990); **Louisiana**, La.R.S. 9:355 (1991); **Maine**, 5 M.R.S. § 7570 (Civil Service Employee Benefits), 24 M.R.S. § 2857 (Insurance) (1990); **Michigan**, M.C.L. § 552.513 (1991) (Divorce); **Minnesota**, Minn. 595.02; **Mississippi**, Miss.Code Ann. § 69-2-47 (1990) (Farm Debt); **Missouri**, § 435.014 R.S.Mo. (1990); **Montana**, Mont.Code Anno., § 80-13-211 (1991); **Nebraska**, R.R.S.Neb. § 2-4812 (1991); **New York**, NY CLS Jud. § 849-b (1992); **North Carolina**, NC Gen.Stat. § 95-36 (1991) (Labor); **North Dakota**, N.D.Cent.Code, § 14-09.1-06 (1991); **Ohio**, ORC Ann. § 2317.02 (1991); **Oregon**, ORS § 36.205 (1989); **Pennsylvania**, 43 P.S. § 21134 (1991); **Utah**, Utah Code Ann. § 78-31b-7 (1992); **Vermont**, 21 V.S.A. § 525 (1991) (Labor); **Washington**, RCWA 2609.015 (1990); **Wisconsin**, Wis.Stat. § 767.11 (1989-1990); **Wyoming**, Wyo.Stat. § 1-43-102 (1991). The laws of the jurisdiction in which the particular statement or evidence is sought to be excluded may be controlling on the issue of confidentiality, rather than the jurisdictional laws of the location in which the mediation occurs.

§ 11.2 Confidentiality—Mediation Privilege

Perhaps the strongest extension of the quest to protect information used in mediation is a privilege established in a few jurisdictions. These states currently are: **Florida**, Fla.Stat. § 44.201 (1990); **Massachusetts**, 1991 Mass.ALS 412; **Minnesota**, Minn. 595.02; **Ohio**, ORC Ann. § 2317.02 (1991); **Oklahoma**, 12 Okl.St. § 1805 (1991); **Oregon**, ORS § 107.600 (1989); and **Washington**, RCWA 7.75.050 (1990). The privilege protects the contents of mediation in the same way that information is protected by other evidentiary privileges, including the lawyer-client and doctor-patient privileges.

Where the mediation privilege is termed as an "absolute" privilege, it protects virtually all contents of mediation and in nearly all circumstances. More limited or "quali-

A Lawyer's Guide to Effective Negotiation and Mediation, CLE edition, is the abridged version of the looseleaf edition designed for use in CLE programs. The section and form numbering from the looseleaf edition have been retained in the CLE edition.

155

fied" privileges need to be analyzed by the relevant adjudicatory body on an ad hoc basis.

Even where a mediation privilege is granted, there may still be questions left unanswered. The most important and practical of these questions is: who can assert the privilege? If the grant of the privilege is not clear, an examination of the purpose behind it should reveal the answer: those for whom the privilege is intended are those who can assert it. Similarly, the party intended to be protected by the privilege is usually the only party who can waive it.

Once the party for whom the privilege is intended raises it, other protectionary provisions may be triggered as well. For example, civil procedure rules may prevent the privileged material from being discovered. Federal Rule of Civil Procedure 26(b)(1) explicitly prevents the discovery of privileged information; many jurisdictions have similar provisions.

§ 11.3 Mediator Liability—The Unresolved Question

Whether a mediator can be held liable for actions that occur within the mediation process remains a difficult one to answer. Some state statutes grant mediators legal immunity; in those jurisdictions which do not have controlling statutes, the issue remains unresolved. The states which currently grant mediators immunity currently include: **Arizona**, A.R.S. § 12–134 (1992); **California**, Civ.Pro.Code § 1297.432 (1991); **Colorado**, C.R.S.A. § 13–22–305 (1991); **Florida**, Fla.Stat. § 44.201 (1990); **Illinois**, Ill.Rev.Stat. ch. 11, par. 4804(b) (1991); **Iowa**, Iowa Code § 679.13 (1989); **Maine**, 4 M.R.S. § 18 (1990); **Montana**, Mont.Code Ann. § 8–13–213 (1991); **Nebraska**, 191 Neb. ALS 90; **New Jersey**, NJ § 32:31–5(m); **New York**, NY CLS Pub.Health § 2974 (1992); **North Dakota**, N.D.Cent.Code § 6–09.10–04.1 (1991); **Oklahoma**, 12 Okl.St. § 1805 (1991); **South Dakota**, S.D.Codified Laws § 54–13–20 (1991); **Utah**, 1991 UT.ALS 75; **Virginia**, Va.Code Ann. § 8.01–581.23 (1991); **Washington**, RCWA 7.7.100 (1990); **Wisconsin**,

A Lawyer's Guide to Effective Negotiation and Mediation, CLE edition, is the abridged version of the looseleaf edition designed for use in CLE programs. The section and form numbering from the looseleaf edition have been retained in the CLE edition.

Wis.Stat. § 93.50 (1989–1990); **Wyoming**, Wyo.Stat. § 1–43–104 (1991).

The unresolved nature of mediator liability should not be a cause for alarm among mediators. The reality of the process is that mediators are rarely sued; overall their risk is far lower than many other professions. Nancy Rogers and Richard Salem, *A Student's Guide to Mediation and the Law* (Matthew Bender, 1987) at 171. Moreover, any lawsuit against a mediator would need to prove damages which are a result of the mediator's conduct, a task very difficult to accomplish in most circumstances. *Id.*, at 175.

Should a party attempt to impose liability on a mediator, he could do so under a number of different legal causes of action. Traditional tort doctrines would be applicable when a party claims that the mediator breached a duty of care that was owed to them. A mediation party/plaintiff would probably also want to try and hold the mediator liable under professional malpractice doctrines by holding the mediator to a higher level of duty.

These tort claims would likely be prefaced upon a breach of trust by the mediator, especially one which could have directly affected the outcome, such as a false claim of neutrality. *Id.*, at 172.

A party could also try to bring a cause of action under contract theory, especially in a case where the mediator had the parties sign an agreement prior to the mediation process. Another basis for a contract claim would be where any promises were made to the parties about the process. Such a claim would seek to hold the mediator liable for breaching an express or implied promise.

A mediator might also be sued under a number of other, unrelated doctrines, including fraud, false advertising, or defamation. Jay Folberg and Allison Taylor, *Mediation: A Comprehensive Guide to Resolving Conflicts Without Litigation* (Jossey–Bass Publishers, 1985) at 231. Obviously, the list of potential claims is limited only by the creativity, ingenuity and anger of the aggrieved mediation party and his lawyer.

§ 11.4 Enforceability of Agreements

Another important legal issue for mediation is whether the agreements produced through it are binding upon or legally enforceable by the parties. This issue is usually raised only when a problem arises with the mediation agreement; i.e., one or more of the parties refuses or is unable to comply with some or all of the terms of the agreement.

Form 11–1 is a Sample Mediation Report and Agreement Form. Certainly, it is difficult to provide a specific guide to drafting because the terms of any given mediation will vary widely among parties and situations. As a general suggestion, the drafters of any mediation agreement would be best advised to follow these guidelines in their writing:

(1) Draft in the present tense. While mediation agreements often look to resolving the present and planning for the future, present tense language will work to retain clarity. For example, "If the Defendant shall fail to make a payment" can be re-written to read "If the Defendant fails to make a payment."

(2) Write actively, not passively. Active voice clarifies who is to do what. For example, "The goods shall be delivered . . ." leaves the issue of who will deliver unclear. Re-write this to state: "Plaintiff shall deliver the goods, or insure that the goods are delivered . . ."

(3) Carefully select words of obligation and authorization. The word "shall" or "must" establishes an undertaking of obligation; "may" establishes the right, privilege or authorization.

Note that use of the present tense will also help clarify the existence of obligation and eliminate the ambiguity that then results if the future voice is used in drafting. For example, "Defendant shall pay the total sum in four installments, each of which shall not be by form of personal check." While the first part of the sentence properly establishes the obligation on the part of the defendant,

A Lawyer's Guide to Effective Negotiation and Mediation, CLE edition, is the abridged version of the looseleaf edition designed for use in CLE programs. The section and form numbering from the looseleaf edition have been retained in the CLE edition.

158

the latter use of "shall" creates an ambiguity in that we cannot place a duty on personal checks. Re-drafting would clarify: "Defendant shall pay the total sum in four installments, but not in the form of personal check."

Fortunately, the incidence of non-compliance for mediated agreements is much lower than that for litigated resolutions. The reason for this is likely their consensual nature. C. McEwen and R. Maiman, "Small Claims Mediation in Maine: An Empirical Assessment," 33 Maine L.Rev. 237, 262 (1981).

Enforceability may be important at the initial stages of mediation as many parties want reassurance that the process will produce a binding agreement, and not one that can easily collapse. This is not to suggest that the results of the mediation must be binding on the parties, only that they will maintain hope that such mutually agreeable terms can be uncovered.

Enforceability is not an issue in some circumstances, such as when the parties create an agreement that they know cannot be legally binding. For example, an agreement created between two businessmen, both of whom know the terms to be legally unenforceable, may nevertheless contain unenforceable terms; perhaps their deal was sufficiently lucrative to offset any risk of non-compliance. Nancy Rogers and Richard Salem, *A Student's Guide to Mediation and the Law* (Matthew Bender, 1987) at 156.

Enforceability may also not be an issue when the mechanisms of compliance, such as litigation, would destroy the long-term relationship between the parties. Mediation assumes that the parties may wish to preserve a pre-existing relationship, which is quite often the case in family mediation or certain business disputes.

Finally, confidentiality is not in issue when the parties accept the mediator's assertion, assuming that there is one, that the settlement is enforceable. This is most likely to occur when the parties are relatively unsophisticated, unrepresented by counsel, or when the level or amount of the dispute is not enough to engender serious

A Lawyer's Guide to Effective Negotiation and Mediation, CLE edition, is the abridged version of the looseleaf edition designed for use in CLE programs. The section and form numbering from the looseleaf edition have been retained in the CLE edition.

thoughts of litigation. Community dispute resolution is one common arena for this unquestioned acceptance of the mediator's word.

Some jurisdictions have statutory provisions that make mediation agreements automatically enforceable in a court of law. There are currently 32 states with such provisions: **Arizona**, A.R.S. § 25–381.17 (reconciliation agreements) (1992); **California**, Cal.Gov.Code § 12964 (1991); **Colorado**, C.R.S.A. § 13–22–308 (1991); **Florida**, Fla.Stat. § 44.201 (1990); **Georgia**, O.C.G.A. § 45–19–36(f) (1991); **Hawaii**, HRS § 515–18 (1991); **Indiana**, Burns Ind.Code Ann. § 15–7–6–19 (1991); **Iowa**, Iowa Code § 601A.15(9) (Civil Rights), § 679B.5, .12 (Labor) (1989); **Kansas**, K.S.A. § 23–602(b) (1990); **Kentucky**, KRS Ann. 344.200(5) (1991); **Louisiana**, La.R.S. 9:354 (1991); **Maine**, 24 M.R.S. § 2858, 13 M.R.S. § 1959 (1990); **Maryland**, Md.Com.Law § 13–402(c) (1991); **Michigan**, MCL § 257.1327(C) (1991); **Minnesota**, Minn.Stat. § 572.35 (1991); **Montana**, Mont.Code Ann. § 39–71–2408(2) (Labor), § 80–13–203 (Farm Debt) (1991); **Nebraska**, R.R.S.Neb. § 48–820 (1991); **Nevada**, Nev.Rev. Stat.Ann. § 118B.250(5), .260 (1991); **New Mexico**, N.M.Stat.Ann. § 28–1–4(B) (1991); **New York**, NY Crim.Proc.Law § 170.55(4), Pub.Health Law § 2973 (1992); **North Dakota**, N.D.Cent.Code § 14–09–1–07 (1991); **Ohio**, ORC Ann. § 3116(E), § 4117.14(F), (H), (I) (1991); **Oklahoma**, 25 Okl.St. § 1505(a), (b), (e) (1991); **Oregon**, ORS § 107.590 (Family), § 659.050(7) (Civil Rights) (1989); **Tennesee**, Tenn.Code Ann. § 4–21–301, 303, 307 (1991); **Texas**, Tx.Civ.Prac. & Rem.Code § 154.024(d) (1991); **Vermont**, 21 V.S.A. § 552(b) (not binding) (1991); **Washington**, RCWA § 7.75.080 (1990); **Wisconsin**, Wis.Stat. § 767.12(a) (1989–1990). These statutory provisions are often limited in their application, and are often contained within the statutory realms of the specific legal area. There may also be limitations upon the enforceability contained either in the statute or in the settlement agreements.

The primary consideration for determining whether a mediation agreement is enforceable is evaluating its va-

A Lawyer's Guide to Effective Negotiation and Mediation, CLE edition, is the abridged version of the looseleaf edition designed for use in CLE programs. The section and form numbering from the looseleaf edition have been retained in the CLE edition.

160

lidity as a contract. Every mediation agreement needs to comply with all the requirements of contract law: it must contain all the elements of a valid contract and it must not be subject to any defenses.

The requisite elements of a valid contract are: an offer, Restatement (Second) of Contracts, Section 21 et seq (1979); an acceptance of the offer, Restatement (Second) of Contracts, Section 41, et seq. (1979); and an exchange of consideration, Restatement (Second) of Contracts, Section 71 et seq. (1979). In addition, the parties must have the appropriate authority and legal capacity to enter into the agreement. If all of these components are met, then the mediation agreement can be considered to be a binding contract.

Because of the unique nature of mediation, certain of these components merit further discussion. First, acceptance implies a mutual meeting of the minds. This does not mean, however, that an imbalanced agreement or one that is signed with less than absolute enthusiasm is *not* binding. In fact, grudging acceptance may be sufficient to create a binding agreement.

Second, the courts will rarely inquire into the adequacy of the consideration; the simple peace of mind produced by this type of resolution may be all that is needed for a court to consider it sufficient consideration.

Finally, the issue of proper authority may arise in certain public sector disputes, particularly environmental ones, if the parties seek to bind non-participants in the process and to the agreement. Such agreements may be considered void as against public policy.

There are a number of potential defenses available to someone who does not want to be bound by a mediation agreement. These defenses include fraud, misrepresentation, or mistake. In reality, they are not likely to succeed absent some sort of egregious result or conduct by a party or mediator.

Impossibility may also be a viable defense in some circumstances, but only if the situation for the parties changes after the mediation is over. Unconscionability

A Lawyer's Guide to Effective Negotiation and Mediation, CLE edition, is the abridged version of the looseleaf edition designed for use in CLE programs. The section and form numbering from the looseleaf edition have been retained in the CLE edition.

161

could also be a useful tactic when there is an extreme power imbalance that produces an unfair result, but since power is a perceived variable, it is not an easy argument to prove.

§ 11.5 Mediation Ethics

Considerations of professional responsibility in mediation are concerned with the role and actions of the mediator. The need and scope of the mediator's neutrality is the most important ethical issue of mediation. Mediators need to project an image of neutrality from the onset of the process; they should not do anything to tarnish this image in the eyes of the parties.

Yet, if most mediators have an interest in bringing the parties to an agreement that is both acceptable and possible to implement, then can they really be considered disinterested in the outcome of the process? While not seemingly a serious concern, mediators need to be certain that their desire to achieve resolution is not imposed on the parties. Rather, the agreement, if any, must emerge from the parties themselves, or the process was not undertaken as it was intended.

A Lawyer's Guide to Effective Negotiation and Mediation, CLE edition, is the abridged version of the looseleaf edition designed for use in CLE programs. The section and form numbering from the looseleaf edition have been retained in the CLE edition.

162

Form 11-1

Sample Mediation Report and Agreement Form

_____

_____   _____

Plaintiff/Petitioner   Attorney

       vs.   NO: _____

_____   _____

_____   _____

Defendant(s)/Respondent(s)   Attorney(s)

                                                    _____

                                                    Mediator

Date of Mediation: _____

Location of Mediation: _____

Issues Presented to the Mediator: _____

_____

_____

Results of the Mediation:

    Recognizing that the purpose of the mediation is to allow the parties the opportunity to resolve their differences in this non-adversarial environment with the assistance of an impartial and independent Mediator, this agreement between the parties is intended to alleviate the need for further outside intervention. At the conclusion of this process:

____   The parties have reached an Agreement, the terms of which are set out below.

____   The parties are unable to reach an Agreement. The issues for further hearing or litigation have been listed.

____   The parties agree to keep the terms of this mediation and/or agreement confidential.

*

Mediation Agreement

The parties have reached a specific agreement. The following terms are intended to resolve the existing dispute between the parties. The terms herein seek to predict what may happen, provide for that contingency and protect the parties with a resolution.

The specific terms of this agreement are as follows:

Plaintiff/Petitioner agrees as follows:

_____

_____

_____

_____

_____

_____

_____

_____

_____

Defendant/Respondent # 1 agrees as follows:

_____

_____

_____

_____

_____

_____

_____

_____

*

Form 11-1 (continued)

Defendant/Respondent # 2 agrees as follows:

_____

_____

_____

_____

_____

_____

_____

_____

_____

In addition, all of the parties jointly agree as follows:

_____

_____

_____

_____

_____

_____

_____

_____

_____

_____

By their signatures, the parties acknowledge that they have read and understand each of the terms stated above. They also acknowledge that they are entering into this

*

agreement freely and acknowledge that its terms are to be carried out in their entirety. In the event of a subsequent conflict, the parties agree to submit the matter to mediation, prior to instituting any legal action based on the terms herein.

Date	Plaintiff/Petitioner	Date	Defendant/Respondent # 1
		Date	Defendant/Respondent # 2
Date	Plaintiff/Petitioner Attorney	Date	Defendant/Respondent Attorney # 1
		Date	Defendant/Respondent Attorney # 2

*

TABLE OF STATUTES AND RULES

TABLE OF STATUTES AND RULES

NORTH DAKOTA CENTURY CODE

Sec.	This Work Sec.
6–09.10–04.1	11.3
14–09.1–06	11.1
14–09.1–07	11.4

OHIO REVISED CODE

Sec.	This Work Sec.
2317.02	11.1
	11.2
3116(E)	11.4
4117.14(F)	11.4
4117.14(H)	11.4
4117.14(I)	11.4

OKLAHOMA STATUTES

Tit.	This Work Sec.
12, § 1805	11.1
	11.2
	11.3
25, § 1505(a)	11.4
25, § 1505(b)	11.4
25, § 1505(e)	11.4

OREGON REVISED STATUTES

Sec.	This Work Sec.
36.205	11.1
107.590	11.4
107.600	11.2
659.050(7)	11.4

PENNSYLVANIA STATUTES

Vol.	This Work Sec.
43, § 21134	11.1

SOUTH DAKOTA CODIFIED LAWS

Sec.	This Work Sec.
54–13–20	11.3

TENNESSEE CODE ANNOTATED

Sec.	This Work Sec.
4–21–301	11.4
4–21–303	11.4
4–21–307	11.4

VERNON'S ANNOTATED TEXAS CIVIL STATUTES

Art.	This Work Sec.
154.053(b)	11.1

V.T.C.A., TEXAS CIVIL PRACTICE & REMEDIES CODE

Sec.	This Work Sec.
154.024(d)	11.4

UTAH CODE ANNOTATED

Sec.	This Work Sec.
78–31b–7	11.1

VERMONT STATUTES ANNOTATED

Tit.	This Work Sec.
21, § 525	11.1
21, § 552(b)	11.4

VIRGINIA CODE

Sec.	This Work Sec.
8.01—581.23	11.3

WEST'S REVISED CODE OF WASHINGTON ANNOTATED

Sec.	This Work Sec.
7.7.100	11.3
7.75.050	11.2
7.75.080	11.4
2609.015	11.1

WISCONSIN STATUTES ANNOTATED

Sec.	This Work Sec.
93.50	11.3
767.11	11.1
767.12(a)	11.4

WYOMING STATUTES

Sec.	This Work Sec.
1–43–102	11.1
1–43–104	11.3

FEDERAL RULES OF CIVIL PROCEDURE

Rule	This Work Sec.
26(b)(1)	11.2

FEDERAL RULES OF EVIDENCE

Rule	This Work Sec.
408	11.1

TABLE OF STATUTES AND RULES

INDEX

References are to Sections

INDEX

INDEX

INDEX

INDEX

179

INDEX

INDEX

INDEX

INDEX

INDEX

INDEX

INDEX

INDEX

INDEX

†